W9-BPK-078

Rick Steves'

SNAPSHOT

Barcelona

CONTENTS

INTRODUCTION

This Snapshot guide, excerpted from the latest edition of my guidebook *Rick Steves' Spain,* introduces you to Barcelona. The capital of the Catalan people, a bustling port for centuries, and one of Spain's leading cities, Barcelona delights its visitors. Stroll the famous Ramblas people-zone and explore the tangled alleys of the Gothic old town. Ogle the mind-bending facades of Antoni Gaudí and other Modernista architects. Marvel at the dynamic arts scene and excellent museums, with top works by former residents Pablo Picasso, Salvador Dalí, and Joan Miró. After dark, enjoy Barcelona's vibrant nightlife as you go bar-hopping to assemble a tasty meal of tapas.

Stretching in both directions from Barcelona is Spain's best bit of Mediterranean coast. Side-trip to the unforgettably weird Salvador Dalí sights at Figueres and Cadaqués, spread out your beach towel at the relaxing resort town of Sitges, or make a pilgrimage to the rugged mountain retreat of Montserrat.

To help you have the best trip possible, I've included the following topics in this book:

• **Planning Your Time,** with advice on how to make the most of your limited time

• **Orientation,** including tourist information (abbreviated as TI), tips on public transportation, local tour options, and helpful hints

• **Sights** with ratings:

▲▲▲—Don't miss

▲▲—Try hard to see

▲—Worthwhile if you can make it

No rating—Worth knowing about

• **Sleeping** and **Eating,** with good-value recommendations in every price range

• **Connections,** with tips on trains, buses, and driving
Practicalities, near the end of this book, has information on money, phoning, hotel reservations, transportation, and more, plus Spanish survival phrases.

To travel smartly, read this little book in its entirety before you go. It's my hope that this guide will make your trip more meaningful and rewarding. Traveling like a temporary local, you'll get the absolute most out of every mile, minute, and euro.

Buen viaje!

Rick Steves

BARCELONA

Barcelona is Spain's second city, and the capital of the proud and distinct region of Catalunya. With Franco's fascism now ancient history, Catalan flags wave once again. And the local language and culture are on a roll in Spain's most cosmopolitan and European corner.

Barcelona bubbles with life in its narrow Barri Gòtic alleys, along the grand boulevards, and throughout the chic, grid-planned, new part of town, called Eixample. While Barcelona had an illustrious past as a Roman colony, Visigothic capital, 14th-century maritime power, and—in more modern times—a top Mediterranean textile and manufacturing center, you'll have more fun if you throw out the history books and just drift through the city. If you're in the mood to surrender to a city's charms, let it be in Barcelona.

Planning Your Time

Located in the far northeast corner of Spain, Barcelona makes a good first or last stop for your trip. With the fast AVE train, Barcelona is three hours away from Madrid. Or you could sandwich Barcelona between flights. From the US, it's as easy to fly into Barcelona as it is to land in Madrid, Lisbon, or Paris. Those who plan on renting a car at some point during their trip can start here first, fly or train to Madrid, and sightsee Madrid and Toledo, all before picking up their car—cleverly saving on several days' worth of rental fees.

On the shortest visit, Barcelona is worth one night, one day, and an evening flight or train ride out. The Ramblas is two different streets by day and by night. Stroll it from top to bottom in the evening and again the next morning, grabbing breakfast on a stool

Barcelona Overview

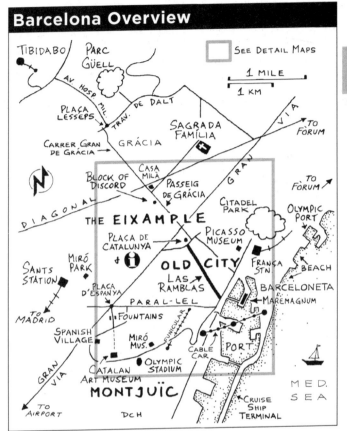

in a market café. Wander the Barri Gòtic (BAH-ree GOH-teek), see the cathedral, and have lunch in the Eixample (eye-SHAM-plah). The top two sights in town, Antoni Gaudí's Sagrada Família church and the Picasso Museum, are usually open until 20:00 during the summer (Picasso closed Mon). Note that if you want to tour the Catalan Concert Hall, with its oh-wow Modernista interior, you'll need to reserve at least two days in advance. The illuminated Magic Fountains on Montjuïc make a good finale for your day.

Of course, Barcelona in a day is insane. To better sample the city's ample charm, spread your visit over two or three days. With two days, you could divide and conquer the town geographically: one day for the Barri Gòtic (Ramblas, cathedral area, Picasso Museum); and another for the Eixample and Gaudí sights (Casa Milà, Sagrada Família, Parc Güell). Do Montjuïc on whichever day you're not exhausted (if any).

With more time, several tempting day trips await nearby—see the Near Barcelona chapter for tips on Montserrat, Sitges, and the Salvador Dalí sights at Figueres and Cadaqués.

Orientation to Barcelona

Like Los Angeles, Barcelona is a basically flat city that sprawls out under the sun between the sea and the mountains. It's huge (1.6 million people, with about 4 million people in greater Barcelona), but travelers need only focus on four areas: the Old City, the harbor/Barceloneta, the Eixample, and Montjuïc.

A large square, Plaça de Catalunya, sits at the center of Barcelona, dividing the older and newer parts of town. Sloping downhill from the Plaça de Catalunya is the Old City, with the boulevard called the Ramblas running down to the harbor. Above Plaça de Catalunya is the modern residential area called the Eixample. The Montjuïc hill overlooks the harbor. Outside the Old City, Barcelona's sights are widely scattered, but with a map and a willingness to figure out the sleek Metro system (or a few euros for taxis), all is manageable.

Here are more details per neighborhood:

The **Old City** is where you'll probably spend most of your time. This is the compact soul of Barcelona—your strolling, shopping, and people-watching nucleus. It's a labyrinth of narrow streets that once were confined by the medieval walls. The lively pedestrian drag called the **Ramblas**—one of Europe's great people-watching streets—runs through the heart of the Old City from Plaça de Catalunya down to the harbor. The Old City is divided into thirds by the Ramblas and another major thoroughfare, Via Laietana. To the west of the Ramblas is the **Raval,** enlivened by its university and modern-art museum. The Raval is of least interest to tourists (and, in fact, some parts of it are quite seedy and should be avoided). Far better is the **Barri Gòtic** (Gothic Quarter), between the Ramblas and Via Laietana, with the cathedral as its navel. To the east of Via Laietana is the trendy **Ribera** district (a.k.a. "El Born"), centered on the Picasso Museum and the Church of Santa Maria del Mar.

The **harborfront** has been energized since the 1992 Olympics. A pedestrian bridge links the Ramblas with the modern Mare-magnum shopping/aquarium complex. On the peninsula across the harbor is **Barceloneta,** a traditional fishing neighborhood

Cheap Tricks in Barcelona

- Arriving by train? Save time, hassle, and the cost of a Metro ride by finding out if your train stops at any of the handy downtown stations (such as Passeig de Gràcia or Plaça de Catalunya). But remember that AVE trains from Madrid stop only at Sants Station.

- If connecting to cities elsewhere in Spain, don't overlook budget flights, which can be cheaper and faster than the train or bus.

- For getting around the city, skip taxis and the Tourist Bus, and instead use the excellent network of Metro and buses. The T10 Card (10 rides for €7.85) makes the system super-cheap—each ride costs €0.78 instead of €1.40 for an individual ticket.

- Use the T10 Card on bus #50, which is cheaper than the hop-on, hop-off bus and gives you a local's tour of Gràcia and Montjuïc.

- If visiting only the cathedral, go when it's free, 8:00–12:45 (until 13:45 on Sun) or 17:15–19:30. But if you want to see the elevator (€2.50), choir (€2.20), and museum (€2), it's better to go when those sights are covered by the €5 cathedral entry. Several interesting sights around the cathedral (such as the Deacon's House and the Roman Temple) are also free to enter, as well as the nearby Church of Santa Maria del Mar in La Ribera.

- One of Barcelona's most delightful Modernista sights, Antoni Gaudí's Parc Güell, is free and an enjoyable place to relax. Some expensive Gaudí sights (such as Casa Milà, Casa Batlló, and the Sagrada Família) can be just as interesting from the outside, without paying the entry fee. For a free glimpse at a Gaudí interior, visit Palau Güell (only part of the building is open during renovation, and it may begin charging admission when it's completed in 2011).

- Some museums have certain days and times when they don't charge admission: the Picasso and City History museums (first Sun of month and Sun afternoon), Catalan Art Museum (first Sun of month), and Frederic Marès Museum (closed for renovation but may reopen in summer of 2011; when open, free Wed and Sun afternoon).

- When tapas-hopping, note that trendy, upscale neighborhoods—such as the Eixample and La Ribera—come with higher prices. For a cheaper and more characteristic meal, find a blue-collar neighborhood (such as Carrer de la Mercè).

that's home to some good seafood restaurants and a string of sandy beaches. Beyond Barceloneta, a man-made beach, several miles long, leads east to the commercial and convention district called the **Fòrum.**

North of the Old City, beyond the bustling hub of Plaça de Catalunya, is the elegant **Eixample** district—its grid plan is softened by cut-off corners. Much of Barcelona's Modernista architecture is found here. To the north is the **Gràcia** district and, beyond that, Antoni Gaudí's **Parc Güell.**

The large hill overlooking the city to the southwest is **Montjuïc,** home to a variety of attractions, including some excellent museums (Catalan Art, Joan Miró) and the Olympic Stadium.

Apart from your geographical orientation, you'll need to orient yourself linguistically to a language distinct from Spanish. Although Spanish ("Castilian"/*castellano*) is widely spoken, the native tongue in this region is Catalan—nearly as different from Spanish as Italian.

Tourist Information

Barcelona's TI has several branches. The main one is at **Plaça de Catalunya** (daily 9:00–21:00, under the main square near recommended hotels—look for red sign, tel. 932-853-832). Other convenient branches include at the top of the **Ramblas** (daily 9:00–21:00, at #115); **Plaça de Sant Jaume,** just south of the cathedral (Mon–Fri 8:30–20:00, Sat 9:00–19:00, Sun 10:00–14:00); **Plaça d'Espanya** (daily July–Sept 10:00–20:00, Oct–June 10:00–16:00); the **airport** (daily 9:00–21:00, offices in both sections A and B of terminal 2); **Sants train station** (Mon–Fri 8:00–20:00, Sat–Sun 8:00–14:00, near track 6); **Nord bus station** (daily July–Sept 9:00–21:00, Oct–June 9:00–15:00); and more. Throughout the summer, young red-jacketed tourist-info helpers appear in the most touristy parts of town. The central information number for all TIs is 932-853-834 (www.barcelonaturisme.cat).

At any TI, pick up the free city map (although the free Corte Inglés map provided by most hotels is better), the small Metro map, and the free quarterly *See Barcelona* guide (practical information on museum hours, restaurants, transportation, history, festivals, and so on). The monthly *Barcelona Metropolitan* magazine and quarterly *What's On Barcelona* (both free and in English) have timely and substantial coverage of topics and events. The *Metro Walks* booklet (€2) details seven city walks combined with Metro rides, including a few interesting outlying neighborhoods. The TI is a handy place to buy tickets for the Tourist Bus (described later, under "Getting Around Barcelona"). Some TIs (at Plaça de Catalunya, Plaça de Sant Jaume, and the airport) also provide a room-booking service.

The main TI, at Plaça de Catalunya, offers guided walks (described later, under "Tours in Barcelona"). Its Modernisme desk gives out a handy route map showing all the Modernista buildings and offers a sightseeing discount package (€12 for a great guidebook and 20 percent discounts to many Modernisme sites—worthwhile if going beyond my big three; for €18 you'll also get a guidebook to Modernista bars and restaurants).

The **all-Catalunya TI** works fine for the entire region, and even Madrid (Mon–Sat 10:00–19:00, Sun 10:00–14:00, on Plaça de Joan Carlos I, at the intersection of Diagonal and Passeig de Gràcia, Passeig de Gràcia 107, tel. 932-388-091).

Articket Card: This ticket includes admission to seven art museums and their temporary exhibits, including the recommended Picasso Museum, Casa Milà, Catalan Art Museum, and Fundació Joan Miró (€22, valid for six months, sold at TIs and participating museums, www.articketbcn.org). If you're planning to go to three or more of the museums, this time-saver pays for itself. To skip the ticket-buying line at a museum, show your Articket Card (to the ticket-taker, at the info desk, or at the group entrance), and you'll get your entrance ticket pronto.

Barcelona Card: This card covers public transportation (buses, Metro, Montjuïc funicular, and *golondrina* harbor tour) and includes free admission to minor sights and discounts on major sights (€25/2 days, €30/3 days, €34/4 days, €40/5 days, sold at TIs and El Corte Inglés department store).

Arrival in Barcelona

By Train: Virtually all trains end up at Barcelona's Sants train station (described below). But be aware that many trains also pass through other stations en route, such as **França Station** (between the Ribera and Barceloneta neighborhoods), or the downtown **Passeig de Gràcia** or **Plaça de Catalunya** stations (which are also Metro stops—and very close to most of my recommended hotels).

Figure out which stations your train stops at, and get off at the one most convenient to your hotel. (AVE trains from Madrid go only to Sants Station.)

Sants Station is vast and sprawling, but manageable. In the large lobby area under the upper tracks, you'll find a TI; ATMs; a world of handy shops and eateries; and a classy, quiet Sala Euromed lounge for travelers with first-class reservations (TV, free drinks, study tables, and coffee bar). Sants is the only Barcelona station with luggage storage (small bag-€3/day, big bag-€4.50/day, requires security check, daily 5:30–23:00, follow signs to *consigna*, at far end of hallway from tracks 13–14).

There's also a long wall of ticket windows. Figure out which is right for you before you wait in line (all are labeled in English). Generally, the first stretch (on the left, windows 1–8) is for local trains, such as to Sitges; the next group (windows 9–21) handles advance tickets for long-distance trains; farther to the right are information windows (22–26)—go here first if you're not sure which window you want; and those at the right end (windows 27–31) sell tickets for long-distance trains leaving today. Attendants are often standing by to help you find the right line. If you know what you want, there are also automated train-ticket vending machines. For long-distance trains, buy tickets at machines labeled *su turno*.

To get into downtown Barcelona from Sants Station, simply follow signs for the Metro. The L3 (green) line zips you directly to a number of useful points in town, including all of my recommended hotels. You also can save time by taking the *cercanías* local trains to Plaça de Catalunya, just five minutes away. Lines C1, C3, C4, or C7, departing from track 8, all take you there. Or when a train is pulling in, look at the red letter board listing the stops—Plaça de Catalunya is the first stop on the list. You can purchase tickets (€1.40) at touch-screen machines near the tracks, or use your T10 Card.

If departing from the downtown **Passeig de Gràcia Station,** where three Metro lines converge with the rail line, you might find the underground tunnels confusing. You can't access the RENFE Station directly from some of the entrances. Use the northern entrances to this station (rather than the southern "Consell de Cent" entrance, which is closest to Plaça de Catalunya).

By Plane: Barcelona's **El Prat de Llobregat Airport,** eight miles southwest of town, has two large terminals: 1 and 2. Terminal 2 is divided into sections A, B, and C. Terminal 1 and the bigger sections of terminal 2 (A and B) each have a post office, a pharmacy, a left-luggage office, plenty of good cafeterias in the gate areas, and ATMs (avoid the gimmicky machines before the baggage carousels; instead, use the bank-affiliated ATMs at the far-left end of the arrivals hall as you face the street). Airport info tel. 913-211-000.

You have two options for getting downtown cheaply and quickly: The **Aerobus** (#A1 and #A2, corresponding with terminals 1 and 2) stops immediately outside the arrivals lobby of both terminals (and in each section of terminal 2). In about 30 minutes, it takes you to downtown, where it makes several stops, including Plaça d'Espanya and Plaça de Catalunya—near many of my recommended hotels (departs every 6 minutes, from airport 6:00–1:00

in the morning, from downtown 5:30–24:15, €5 one-way, €8.65 round-trip, buy ticket from machine or from driver, tel. 934-156-020). The line to board the bus can be very long, but—thanks to the high frequency of buses—it moves fast.

The second option from terminal 2 is the RENFE *cercanías* **train,** which involves more walking. Head down the long orange-roofed overpass between sections A and B to reach the station (line 2, 2/hour at about :08 and :38 past the hour, 20 minutes to Sants Station, 25 minutes to Passeig de Gràcia Station—near Plaça de Catalunya and many recommended hotels, 30 minutes to França Station; €3 or covered by T10 Card, which you can purchase at automated machines at the airport train station). Long-term plans call for the RENFE *cercanías* train and eventually the AVE to be extended to terminal 1, and for the Metro's line 9 to be extended to both terminals 1 and 2. Stay tuned.

A **taxi** between the airport and downtown costs about €30.

Some budget airlines, including Ryanair, use **Girona–Costa Brava Airport,** located 60 miles north of Barcelona near Girona. Sagalés buses link to Barcelona (departures timed to meet flights, 1.25 hours, €12, tel. 935-931-300 or 902-361-550, www.sagales .com). You can also go to Girona on a Sagalés bus (hourly, 25 minutes, €3) or a taxi (€25), then catch a train to Barcelona (at least hourly, 1.25 hours, €15–20). A taxi between the Girona airport and Barcelona costs at least €120. Airport info tel. 972-186-600.

By Car: Barcelona's parking fees are outrageously expensive (the lot behind La Boquería market charges upward of €25/day). You won't need a car in Barcelona, because the taxis and public transportation are so good.

By Cruise Ship: Several major cruise lines (including Royal Caribbean, Norwegian, Princess, and Disney) come into Barcelona's Puerto del Muelle Adosado. Each of its four terminals (A–D) has a cafe, security checkpoint, waiting room, check-in desks, bus stop, and taxi stand. It's about 1.5 miles to the city center—easiest by taxi (10–15 minutes, €10 to the Ramblas, €15 to Plaça de Catalunya). Legal supplements are posted on the taxi window: €2.10 port fee and €1/bag. Taxis meet each arriving ship and are waiting as you exit the terminal building. During high season (May–Sept), when as many as six ships dock on the same day, the ride can take twice as long and cost €10 more.

An alternative is to take the blue port-run Lanzadera bus from the terminal parking lot (follow *Public Bus* signs) to the Columbus Monument at the bottom of the Ramblas, near the Metro Drassanes stop (€3 round-trip, €2 one-way, buses leave every 20–30 minutes, timed to cruise ship arrival, tel. 932-986-000). From there you can walk or Metro to your destination.

Helpful Hints

Theft Alert: You're more likely to be pickpocketed here—especially on the Ramblas—than about anywhere else in Europe. Most of the crime is nonviolent, but muggings do occur. Leave valuables in your hotel and wear a money belt.

Street scams are easy to avoid if you recognize them. Most common is the too-friendly local who tries to engage you in conversation by asking for the time, talking sports, asking whether you speak English, and so on. Beware of thieves posing as lost tourists who ask for your help. A typical street gambling scam is the pea-and-carrot game, a variation on the shell game. The people winning are all ringers, and you can be sure that you'll lose if you play. Also beware of groups of women aggressively selling carnations, people offering to clean off a stain from your shirt, and people picking things up in front of you on escalators. If you stop for any commotion or show on the Ramblas, put your hands in your pockets before someone else does. Assume any scuffle is simply a distraction by a team of thieves. Crooks are inventive, so keep your guard up. Don't be intimidated...just be smart.

Some areas feel seedy and can be unsafe after dark; I'd avoid the southern part of the Barri Gòtic (basically the two or three blocks directly south and east of Plaça Reial—though the strip near the Carrer de la Mercè tapas bars is better), and I wouldn't venture too deep into the Raval (just west of the Ramblas). One block can separate a comfy tourist zone from the junkies and prostitutes.

US Consulate: It's at Passeig Reina Elisenda 23 (passport services Mon–Fri 9:00–13:00, closed Sat–Sun, tel. 932-802-227).

Emergency Phone Numbers: General emergencies—112, police—092, ambulance—061 or 112.

Internet Access: Navega Web has hundreds of computers for accessing the Internet and burning pictures onto a disk. It's conveniently located across from La Boquería market, downstairs in the bright Centre Comercial New Park (daily 10:00–24:00, Ramblas 88–94, tel. 933-179-193).

Pharmacy: A 24-hour pharmacy is near La Boquería market at #98 on the Ramblas.

Laundry: Several self-service launderettes are located around the Old City. **Wash 'n Dry** is on the edge of the tourist zone, near a seedy neighborhood just down the street past the Palau Güell (self-service: wash-€5/load, dry-€2/load, daily 7:00–22:00; full-service: €15/load, daily 9:00–22:00; Carrer Nou de la Rambla 19, tel. 934-121-953).

Bike Rental: Biking is a joy in Citadel Park and along the beach—but it's stressful in the city center, where pedestrians and cars rule. There are plenty of bike-rental places around Citadel Park and La Ribera's Church of Santa Maria del Mar. The handy **Un Cotxe Menys** ("One Car Less"), near the Church of Santa Maria del Mar (50 yards behind the flame memorial), rents bikes and gives out maps and suggested biking routes (€5/hour, €10/4 hours, daily 10:00–19:00, leave €150 or photo ID for deposit, Esparteria 3, tel. 932-682-105, www.bicicletabarcelona.com); they also lead bike tours (see "Tours in Barcelona," later). To rent a bike on the Barceloneta beach, consider **Biciclot** (€6/hour, €13/3 hours, €18/24 hours; summer Mon–Thu 10:00–15:00 & 16:00–20:00, Fri–Sun 10:00–15:00 & 16:00–21:00; off-season Sat–Sun only; on the sand 300 yards from Olympic Village towers at Passeig Maritime 33, tel. 932-219-778). Closer to downtown, **Barcelona Rent-A-Bike** is three blocks downhill from Plaça de Catalunya (€6/2 hours, €10/4 hours, €15/24 hours, daily 9:00–20:00, inside the courtyard at Carrer dels Tallers 45, tel. 933-171-970).

Getting Around Barcelona

By Metro: Barcelona's Metro, among Europe's best, connects just about every place you'll visit. Rides cost €1.40. The T10 Card is a great deal—€7.85 gives you 10 rides (cutting the per-ride cost nearly in half), and the card is shareable. It's good on all Metro and local bus lines as well as the RENFE train lines (including rides to the airport and train station) and the suburban FGC lines (with service to Montserrat). Full- and multi-day passes are also available (€5.90/1 day, €11.20/2 days, €15.90/3 days, €20.40/4 days, €24.10/5 days, www.tmb.cat). Automated machines at the Metro entrance

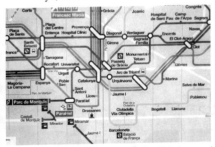

have English instructions and sell all types of tickets (these can be temperamental about accepting bills, so try to have change on hand).

Pick up the free Metro map (at any TI) and study it to get familiar with the system. There are several color-coded lines, but most useful for tourists is the **L3 (green) line;** if you're sticking to my recommended sights and neighborhoods, you'll barely have use for any other. Handy city-center stops on this line include (in order):

Sants Estació—Main train station

Espanya—Plaça d'Espanya, with access to the lower part of Montjuïc and trains to Montserrat

Paral-lel—Funicular to top of Montjuïc

Drassanes—Bottom of the Ramblas, near Maritime Museum, Maremagnum mall, and the cable car up to Montjuïc

Liceu—Middle of the Ramblas, near the heart of the Barri Gòtic and cathedral

Plaça de Catalunya—Top of the Ramblas and main square with TI, airport bus, and lots of transportation connections

Passeig de Gràcia—Classy Eixample street at the Block of Discord; also connection to L2 (purple) line to Sagrada Família and L4 (yellow) line (described below)

Diagonal—Gaudí's Casa Milà

Lesseps—Walk or catch bus #24 to Gaudí's Parc Güell

The **L4 (yellow) line,** which crosses the L3 (green) line at Passeig de Gràcia, is also useful. Helpful stops include **Jaume I** (between the Barri Gòtic/cathedral and La Ribera/Picasso Museum) and **Barceloneta** (at the south end of the Ribera, near the harbor action).

When you enter the Metro, first look for your line number and color, then follow signs to take that line in the direction you're going. Insert your ticket into the turnstile (with the arrow pointing in), then reclaim it. On board, most trains have handy Metro-line diagrams with dots that light up next to upcoming destinations. Because the lines cross one another multiple times, there can be several ways to make any one journey. (It's a good idea to keep a general map with you—especially if you're transferring.) Watch your valuables. If I were a pickpocket, I'd set up shop along the made-for-tourists L3/green line.

By Public Bus: Given the excellent Metro service, it's unlikely you'll take a local bus (also €1.40 or covered by T10 Card, insert ticket in machine behind driver), although I've noted places where the bus makes sense. In particular, bus #50 is good for a tour of Gràcia and Montjuïc.

By Tourist Bus: The handy hop-on, hop-off Tourist Bus (Bus Turístic) offers three multi-stop circuits in colorful double-decker buses that go topless in sunny weather. The two-hour red route covers north Barcelona (most Gaudí sights); the two-hour blue route covers south Barcelona (Barri Gòtic, Montjuïc); and the shorter, 40-minute green route covers the beaches and Fòrum. All have headphone commentary (44 stops, daily 9:00–22:00 in summer, 9:00–21:00 in winter, buses run every 5–25 minutes, most frequent in summer, no green route Oct–March). Ask for a brochure (includes city map) at

the TI or at a pick-up point. One-day (€22) and two-day (€29) tickets, which you can buy on the bus or at the TI, offer 10–20 percent discounts on the city's major sights and walking tours, which will likely save you about the equivalent of half the cost of the Tourist Bus (www.barcelonabusturistic.cat).

By Taxi: Barcelona is one of Europe's best taxi towns. Taxis are plentiful (there are more than 10,000) and honest (whether they like it or not—the light on top shows which tariff they're charging). They're also reasonable (€2 drop charge, €1/kilometer, these "*Tarif 2*" rates are in effect 7:00–21:00, pay higher "*Tarif 1*" rates off-hours, luggage-€1/piece, other fees posted in window). Save time by hopping a cab (figure €10 from Ramblas to Sants Station).

Tours in Barcelona

Walking Tours—The TI at Plaça de Catalunya offers great guided walks through the **Barri Gòtic** in English only (€12.50, daily at 10:00, 2 hours, groups limited to 35, buy your ticket 15 minutes early at the TI desk—not from the guide, in summer call ahead to reserve, tel. 932-853-832, www.barcelonaturisme.cat). A local guide will explain the medieval story of the city as you walk from Plaça de Catalunya through the cathedral neighborhood, finishing at City Hall on Plaça de Sant Jaume. The TI also offers a **Picasso** walk, taking you through the streets of his youth and early career and finishing in the Picasso Museum (€18, includes museum admission; Tue, Thu, and Sat at 16:00; 2 hours plus museum visit). There are also **gourmet** walks (€19, Fri and Sat at 10:00, 2 hours) and **Modernisme** walks (€12.50, Fri and Sat June–Sept at 18:00, Oct–May at 16:00, 2 hours). All tours depart from the TI at Plaça de Catalunya.

Guided Bus Tours—The Barcelona Guide Bureau offers several sightseeing tours leaving from Plaça de Catalunya. Departure times can vary—confirm locally. The **Gaudí** tour visits the facades of Casa Batlló and Casa Milà, as well as Parc Güell and the Sagrada Família (€45, includes Sagrada Família admission, daily at 9:00, also at 15:15 mid-April–Oct, 3 hours). Other tours offered year-round include the **Montjuïc** tour (€33, includes Spanish Village admission, daily at 12:00, 3 hours); the **All Barcelona Highlights** tour (€60, includes Sagrada Família and Spanish Village admissions, daily at 9:00, 6 hours); and the **Montserrat** tour (€40, daily at 15:00, 4 hours), which offers a convenient way to get to this mountaintop monastery if you don't want to deal with public transportation (see Near Barcelona chapter). From April through October, there's also the **Gaudí Beyond the City** tour of "off-the-beaten-path masterpieces" (€30, daily at 12:30, 3 hours); and—for soccer fans—the **Barça** tour, which takes you to the Camp Nou

"You're not in Spain, You're in Catalunya!"

This is a popular nationalistic refrain you might see on T-shirts or stickers around town. Catalunya is *not* the land of bullfighting and flamenco that many visitors envision when they think of Spain (best to wait until you're in Madrid or Sevilla for those).

The region of Catalunya—with Barcelona as its capital—has its own language, history, and culture, and the people have a proud, independent spirit. Historically, Catalunya ("Cataluña" in Spanish, sometimes spelled "Catalonia" in English) has often been at odds with the central Spanish government in Madrid. The Catalan language and culture were discouraged or even outlawed at various times in Spanish history, as Catalunya often chose the wrong side in wars and rebellions against the kings in Madrid. In the Spanish Civil War (1936–1939), Catalunya was one of the last pockets of democratic resistance against the military coup of the fascist dictator Francisco Franco, who punished the region with four decades of repression. During that time, the Catalan flag was banned—but locals vented their national spirit by flying their football team's flag instead.

Three of Barcelona's monuments are reminders of Franco-era suppression. Citadel Park (Parc de la Ciutadella) was originally a much-despised military citadel, constructed in the 18th century to keep locals in line. The Castle of Montjuïc, built for similar reasons, has been the site of numerous political executions, including hundreds during the Franco era. The Sacred Heart Church atop Tibidabo, completed under Franco, was meant to atone for the sins of Barcelonans during the Spanish Civil War—the main sin being opposition to Franco. Although rivalry between Barcelona and Madrid has calmed down in recent times, it rages any time the two cities' football clubs meet.

stadium (€35, daily at 15:15, 3 hours). You can get detailed information and book tickets at a TI, on their website, or simply by showing up at their departure point on Plaça de Catalunya in front of the Hard Rock Café—look for the guides holding orange umbrellas. Buying tickets online can save you a few euros—usually about 10 percent (tel. 933-152-261, www.barcelonaguidebureau.com).

Bus #50 Self-Guided Tour—Combining public bus #50 with a T10 Card gives you an inexpensive tour through Gràcia and Montjuïc. You can catch bus #50 at the Sagrada Família stop (on the Nativity facade side). Once aboard, you'll wind through

To see real Catalan culture, look for the *sardana* dance or an exhibition of *castellers*. These teams of human-castle builders come together for festivals throughout the year to build towers of flesh that can reach more than 50 feet high, topped off by the bravest member of the team—a child! The Gràcia festival in August and the Mercè festival in September are good times to catch the *castellers*.

The Catalan language is irrevocably tied to the history and spirit of the people here. Since the end of the Franco era in the mid-1970s, the language has made a huge resurgence. Now most school-age children learn Catalan first and Spanish second. Although Spanish is understood here (and the basic survival words are the same), Barcelona speaks Catalan.

Here are the essential Catalan phrases:

English	Catalan	Pronounced
Hello	*Hola*	OH-lah
Please	*Si us plau*	see oos plow
Thank you	*Gracies*	GRAH-see-es
Goodbye	*Adéu*	ah-DAY-oo
Exit	*Sortida*	sor-TEE-dah
Long live Catalunya!	*¡Visca Catalunya!*	BEE-skah kah-tah-LOON-yah

Most place names in this chapter are listed in Catalan. Here's a pronunciation guide:

Plaça de Catalunya	PLAS-sah duh cat-ah-LOON-yah
Eixample	eye-SHAM-plah
Passeig de Gràcia	PAH-sage duh grass-EE-ah
Catedral	KAH-tah-dral
Barri Gòtic	BAH-ree GOH-teek
Montjuïc	MOHN-jew-eek

Gràcia's streets down to the Gran Via de les Corts Catalanes, crossing the Passeig de Gràcia (a block away from Plaça de Catalunya). Enjoy the long blocks of Gràcia until you reach Plaça d'Espanya, where on the right you'll see Barcelona's bullring (which is being turned into a mall). You'll go through the two towers of Plaça d'Espanya, with the Catalan Art Museum on the hill in front of you. Then you'll loop through the hills of Montjuïc, passing the Spanish Village, the site of the '92 Olympics (with the communications tower and stadium), the Fundació Joan Miró, and the funicular and cable car up to the Castle of Montjuïc. The end of the line is

Barcelona at a Glance

▲▲▲**Ramblas** Barcelona's colorful, gritty, tourist-filled pedestrian thoroughfare. **Hours:** Always open. See page 18.

▲▲▲**Picasso Museum** Extensive collection offering insight into the brilliant Spanish artist's early years. **Hours:** Tue–Sun 10:00–20:00, closed Mon. See page 34.

▲▲▲**Sagrada Família** Gaudí's remarkable, unfinished cathedral. **Hours:** Daily April–Sept 9:00–20:00, Oct–March 9:00–18:00. See page 47.

▲▲**City History Museum** One-stop trip through town history, from Roman times to today. **Hours:** Tue–Sat April–Sept 10:00–20:00, Oct–March 10:00–14:00 & 16:00–19:00, Sun 10:00–20:00, closed Mon. See page 33.

▲▲**Catalan Concert Hall** Best Modernista interior in Barcelona. **Hours:** 50-minute English tours daily every hour 10:00–15:00, plus frequent concerts. See page 39.

▲▲**Casa Milà** Barcelona's quintessential Modernista building, the famous melting-ice-cream Gaudí creation. **Hours:** Daily March–Oct 9:00–20:00, Nov–Feb 9:00–18:30. See page 44.

▲▲**Catalan Art Museum** World-class collection of this region's art, including a substantial Romanesque collection. **Hours:** Tue–Sat 10:00–19:00, Sun 10:00–14:30, closed Mon. See page 57.

▲**Maritime Museum** Housed in an impressive medieval shipyard, it's a sailor's delight. **Hours:** Some exhibits closed for renovation, others daily 10:00–20:00. See page 28.

▲**Columbus Monument** Elevator ride to the best easy view in town. **Hours:** Daily May–Oct 9:00–20:30, Nov–April 10:00–18:30. See page 29.

about a block away from the funicular. From here you can walk back to the Joan Miró or Catalan Art museums; or continue in the direction of the bus route down the hill to a different cable car, which takes you to the Barceloneta area.

Bike Tours—Several companies run bike tours around Barcelona. **Un Cotxe Menys** ("One Car Less") organizes three-hour English-only bike tours daily at 11:00 (April–mid-Sept also Fri–Mon at 16:30). Your guide leads you from sight to sight, mostly on bike paths and through parks, with a stop-and-go commentary (€22

▲**Cathedral of Barcelona** Colossal Gothic cathedral ringed by distinctive chapels. **Hours:** Daily 8:00–12:45 (until 13:45 on Sun) and 17:15–19:30. See page 29.

▲*Sardana* **Dances** Patriotic dance in which proud Catalans join hands in a circle. **Hours:** Every Sun at 12:00, usually also Sat at 18:00. See page 32.

▲**Church of Santa Maria del Mar** Catalan Gothic church in La Ribera, built by wealthy medieval shippers. **Hours:** Daily 9:00–13:30 & 16:30–20:00. See page 39.

▲**Barcelona's Beach** Fun-filled, man-made stretch of sand reaching from the harbor to the Fòrum. **Hours:** Always open. See page 41.

▲**Block of Discord** Noisy block of competing Modernista facades by Gaudí and his rivals. **Hours:** Always viewable. See page 45.

▲**Palau Güell** Exquisitely curvy Gaudí interior. **Hours:** Tue–Sat 10:00–14:30, closed Sun–Mon. See page 47.

▲**Parc Güell** Colorful park at the center of an unfinished Gaudí-designed housing project. **Hours:** Daily 10:00–20:00. See page 52.

▲**Fundació Joan Miró** World's best collection of works by Catalan modern artist Joan Miró. **Hours:** Tue–Sat July–Sept 10:00–20:00, Oct–June 10:00–19:00, Thu until 21:30, Sun 10:00–14:30, closed Mon. See page 55.

▲**Magic Fountains** Lively fountains near Plaça d'Espanya. **Hours:** Almost always May–Sept Thu–Sun 21:00–23:30, no shows Mon–Wed; Oct–April Fri–Sat 19:00–21:00, no shows Sun–Thu. See page 58.

includes bike rental and drink, no reservations needed—just show up at Plaça de Sant Jaume, next to the TI, tel. 932-682-105, www .biketoursbarcelona.com; also see bike-rental listing earlier, under "Helpful Hints").

Local Guides—The Barcelona Guide Bureau is a co-op with about 20 local guides who give personalized four-hour tours (weekdays-€208, per-person price drops as group gets bigger; weekends and holidays-€248, no price break with size of group); **Joana Wilhelm** and **Carles Picazo** are excellent (Via Laietana

54, tel. 932-682-422 or 933-107-778, www.bgb.es). **Jose Soler** is a great and fun-to-be-with local guide who enjoys tailoring a walk through his hometown to your interests (€195/half-day per group, mobile 615-059-326, www.pepitotours.com, info@pepitotours .com).

Self-Guided Walks

Most visitors to Barcelona spend much of their time in the twisty, atmospheric Old City. These two walks will give meaning to your wandering. The first begins at Barcelona's main square and leads you down the city's main drag through one of Europe's best public spaces: the Ramblas. The second walk starts at the same square but guides you into the heart of the Barri Gòtic, to the neighborhood around Barcelona's impressive cathedral.

▲▲▲The Ramblas Ramble:
From Plaça de Catalunya down the Ramblas

Barcelona's central square and main boulevard exert a powerful pull. Many visitors spend the majority of their time doing laps on the Ramblas. While the allure of the Ramblas is fading (as tacky tourist shops and fast-food joints replace its former elegance), this is still a fun people zone that offers a good introduction to the city. See it, but be sure to venture farther afield. Here's a top-to-bottom orientation walk.

Plaça de Catalunya: This vast central square divides old and new Barcelona. It's also the hub for the Metro, bus, airport shuttle, and Tourist Bus (red northern route leaves from El Corte Inglés—described below; blue southern route leaves from the west, or Ramblas, side of the square). Overlooking the square, the huge **El Corte Inglés** department store offers everything from bonsai trees to a travel agency, plus one-hour photo developing, haircuts, and cheap souvenirs (Mon–Sat 10:00–22:00, closed Sun, pick up English directory flier, supermarket in basement, ninth-floor terrace cafeteria/restaurant has great city view—take elevator from entrance nearest the TI, tel. 933-063-800). Across the square from El Corte Inglés is **FNAC,** a French department store popular for electronics, music, and books (on west side of square—behind blue Tourist Bus stop; Mon–Sat 10:00–22:00, closed Sun).

Four great boulevards radiate from Plaça de Catalunya: the Ramblas; the fashionable Passeig de Gràcia (top shops, noisy with traffic); the cozier, but still fashionable, Rambla de Catalunya

The Ramblas Ramble

- ▨ Ramblas
- Ⓜ Metro Station
- Ⓑ Bus Stop

NOT TO SCALE –
PLAÇA DE CATALUNYA TO COLUMBUS
MONUMENT IS A 30 MIN. WALK

TO BLOCK OF DISCORD

PASSEIG DE GRÀCIA

BLUE TOURIST BUS

RAMBLA DE CATALUNYA

FNAC DEP'T. STORE

FGC TRAIN INFO

CAFÉ ZÜRICH

PLAÇA DE CATALUNYA
Catalunya ⓘ

EL CORTE INGLÉS DEP'T. STORE

CANALETES FOUNTAIN

❶ BIRDS

SANTA ANNA

AV. PORTAL DE L'ANGEL

AEROBUS, RED TOURIST BUS & TAXIS

ACADEMY OF SCIENCE

❷

CANUDA

ROMAN NECROPOLIS

CAFÉ GRANJA VIADER

BAROQUE CHURCH

❸

CARME

Liceu Ⓜ

PORTAFERRISSA

CULTURAL INFO PALAU DE LA VIRREINA

FLOWER

PHARMACY
CIGARS

EROTIC MUSEUM

LA BOQUERÍA MARKET

❹

CARDENAL

"UMBRELLA" BLDG.

HOSP.

MIRÓ MOSAIC

BOQ.

BARRI XINES

S. PAV.

FERRAN

TO PLAÇA DE S. JAUME

LICEU OPERA HOUSE

Ⓜ Liceu

PLAÇA REIAL

❺

NOU RAMBLA

Ⓜ Drassanes

PALAU GÜELL

L'ARC

❻

HERBOLARI FERRAN

ESCUDELLERS

MARITIME MUSEUM

COLUMBUS MONUMENT

TO BARCELO-NETA

PASSEIG COLÓM

PICNIC SPOT

DCH

GOLONDRINAS BOATS

HARBOR

RAMBLA DE MAR

TO MAREMAGNUM

❶ The Top of the Ramblas
❷ Rambla of the Little Birds
❸ Baroque Church
❹ La Boquería
❺ Plaça Reial
❻ Bottom of the Ramblas

(most pedestrian-friendly); and the stubby, shop-filled and delightfully traffic-free Avinguda Portal de l'Angel. Homesick Americans can even find a Hard Rock Café. Locals traditionally start or end a downtown rendezvous at the venerable Café Zürich (at the corner near the Ramblas).

• *Cross the street from the café to...*

❶ The Top of the Ramblas: Begin your ramble 20 yards down at the ornate fountain (near #129). More than a Champs-Elysées, this grand boulevard takes you from rich (at the top) to rough (at the port) in a one-mile, 30-minute stroll. You'll raft the river of Barcelonan life past a grand opera house, elegant cafés, retread prostitutes, brazen pickpockets, power-dressing con men, artists, street mimes, an outdoor bird market, great shopping, and people looking to charge more for a shoeshine than what you paid for the shoes.

Grab a bench and watch the scene. Open up your map and read some history into it: You're about to walk right across medieval Barcelona, from Plaça de Catalunya to the harbor. Notice

how the higgledy-piggledy street plan of the medieval town was contained within the old town walls—now gone, but traced by a series of roads named Ronda (meaning "to go around"). Find the Roman town, occupying about 10 percent of what became the medieval town—with tighter roads yet around the cathedral. The sprawling modern grid plan beyond the Ronda roads is from the 19th century. Breaks in this urban waffle show where a little town was consumed by the growing city. The popular Passeig de Gràcia was literally the "Road to Gràcia" (once a separate town, now a characteristic Barcelona neighborhood).

Rambla means "stream" in Arabic. The Ramblas used to be a drainage ditch along the medieval wall that once defined what's now called the Barri Gòtic (Gothic Quarter). "Ramblas" is plural, a succession of five separately named segments, but address numbers treat it as a single long street. (In fact, street signs label it as "La Rambla," singular.) Because no streets cross the Ramblas, it has a great pedestrian feel.

You're at Rambla Canaletes, named for the fountain. The black-and-gold **Fountain of Canaletes** is the starting point for celebrations and demonstrations. Legend says that a drink from the fountain ensures that you'll return to Barcelona one day. All along the Ramblas, you'll see newspaper stands (open 24 hours, selling phone cards) and ONCE booths (selling lottery tickets that support Spain's organization of the blind, a powerful advocate for the needs of people with disabilities).

Got some change? As you wander downhill, drop coins into the cans of the human statues (the money often kicks them into entertaining gear). If you take a photo, it's considered good etiquette to drop in a coin. Warning: Wherever people stop to gawk, pickpockets are at work.

• *Walk 100 yards downhill to #115 and the...*

❷ **Rambla of the Little Birds:** Traditionally, kids bring their parents here to buy pets, especially on Sundays. Apartment-dwellers find birds, turtles, and fish easier to handle than dogs and

cats. If you're walking by at night, you'll hear the sad sounds of little tweety birds locked up in their collapsed kiosks.

Along the Ramblas, build-ings with balconies that have flowers are generally living spaces; balconies with air-conditioners generally indicate offices. The Academy of Science's clock (at #115) marks official Barcelona time—synchronize.

The Carrefour Express supermarket has cheap groceries (at #113, Mon–Sat 10:00–22:00, closed Sun, shorter checkout lines in back of store).

A recently discovered **Roman necropolis** is in a park across the street from the bird market, 50 yards behind the big, mod-ern Citadines Hotel (go through the passageway at #122). Local apartment-dwellers blew the whistle on contractors, who hoped they could finish their building before anyone noticed the antiqui-ties they had unearthed. Imagine the tomb-lined road leading into the Roman city of Barcino 2,000 years ago.

• *Another 50 yards takes you to Car-rer del Carme (at #105), and a...*

❸ **Baroque Church:** The big Betlem church fronting the boulevard is Baroque, unusual in Barcelona. Note the Baroque-style sloping roofline, ball-topped pinnacles, and the scrolls above the entrance. And though

Barcelona's Gothic age was rich (with buildings to prove it), the Baroque age hardly left a mark. (The city's importance dropped when New World discoveries shifted lucrative trade to ports on the Atlantic.)

For a sweet treat, head down the narrow lane behind the church (going uphill parallel to the Ramblas about 30 yards) to the recommended **Café Granja Viader,** which has specialized in baked and dairy delights since 1870.

• *Continue down the boulevard and stroll through the Ramblas of Flowers to the Metro stop marked by the red* M *(near #96), where you'll find...*

❹ **La Boquería:** This lively produce market is an explosion of chicken legs, bags of live snails, stiff fish, delicious oranges, and sleeping dogs (Mon–Sat 8:00–20:00, best mornings after 9:00, closed Sun, at #91). Originally outside the walls (as many medieval markets were), it expanded into the colonnaded courtyard of a now-gone monastery. Wander around—as local architect Antoni Gaudí used to—and gain inspiration. The Francesc Conserves shop sells 25 kinds of olives (straight in, near back on right, 100-gram minimum). Full

legs of ham *(jamón serrano)* abound; *Paleta Ibérica de Bellota* hams are the best, and cost about €120 each. Beware: *Huevos del toro* are bull testicles—surprisingly inexpensive...and oh so good. Drop by a café for an *espresso con leche* or breakfast *tortilla española* (potato omelet).

For a quick bite, visit the recommended **Pinotxo Bar** (just to the right as you enter the market), where animated Juan and his family are busy feeding shoppers. (Getting Juan to crack a huge smile and a thumbs-up for your camera makes a great shot...and he loves it.) The stools nearby are a fine perch for enjoying both your coffee and the people-watching. The market and lanes nearby are busy with tempting little eateries.

• *Now turn your attention across the boulevard.*

The **Museum of Erotica** is your standard European sex museum (€9, daily 10:00–20:00, across from market at #96).

To the left, at #100, **Gimeno** sells cigars (appreciate the dying art of cigar boxes). Go ahead, do something forbidden in America but perfectly legal here...buy a Cuban (little singles for less than €1). Tobacco shops sell stamps and phone cards—and plenty of bongs and marijuana gear (the Spanish approach to pot is very casual).

Fifty yards farther, underfoot in the center of the Ramblas, find the much-trod-upon **anchor mosaic**—a reminder of the city's attachment to the sea. Created by noted abstract artist Joan Miró, it marks the midpoint of the Ramblas. (The towering Columbus Monument in the distance—hidden by trees—is at the end of this walk.)

Continue a few more steps down to the **Liceu Opera House.** From the Opera House, cross the Ramblas to Café de l'Opera for a beverage (#74). This bustling café, with Modernista decor and a historic atmosphere, boasts that it's been open since 1929, even during the Spanish Civil War.

• *Continue down the Ramblas to #46; turn left down an arcaded lane (Correr de Colom) to a square filled with palm trees.*

❺ Plaça Reial: This elegant Neoclassical square has a colonial (or maybe post-colonial) ambience. It comes complete with old-fashioned taverns, modern bars with patio seating, a Sunday coin-and-stamp market (10:00–14:00), Gaudí's first public works (the two colorful helmeted lamp-posts), and characters who don't need the palm trees to be shady. **Herbolari Ferran** is a fine and aromatic shop of herbs, with fun souvenirs such as top-quality saffron, or *safra* (Mon–Fri 9:30–14:00 & 16:30–20:00, closed Sat–Sun, downstairs at Plaça Reial 18—to the right as you enter the square). The small streets stretching toward the water from the square are intriguing, but less safe.

Back on the other side of the Ramblas, **Palau Güell** offers an enjoyable look at a Gaudí interior (Carrer Nou de la Rambla 3, partly closed for renovation in 2011). This apartment was the first of Gaudí's innovative buildings, with a parabolic front doorway that signaled his emerging nonrectangular style.

• *Continue farther downhill on the Ramblas.*

❻ Bottom of the Ramblas: The neighborhood on the right-hand side, Barri Xines, is the world's only Chinatown with nothing even remotely Chinese in or near it. Named for the prejudiced notion that Chinese immigrants go hand-in-hand with poverty, prostitution, and drug dealing, the neighborhood's actual inhabitants are poor Spanish, North African, and Roma (Gypsy) people. At night, the Barri Xines is frequented by prostitutes, many of them transvestites, who cater to sailors wandering up from the port. Prostitution is nothing new here. Check out the thresholds at #22 and #24 (along the left side of the Ramblas)—with holes worn in long ago by the heels of anxious ladies.

The bottom of the Ramblas is marked by the city's giant medieval shipyards (on the right, now the Maritime Museum—partly closed for restoration through 2013) and the Columbus Monument. Just beyond the Columbus Monument, **La Rambla del**

Mar ("Rambla of the Sea") is a modern extension of the boulevard into the harbor. A popular wooden pedestrian bridge—with waves like the sea—leads to Maremagnum, a soulless Spanish mall with a cinema, a huge aquarium, restaurants, and piles of people. Late at night, it's a rollicking youth hangout. It's a worthwhile stroll.

▲▲The Barri Gòtic: From Plaça de Catalunya to the Cathedral

Barcelona's Barri Gòtic, or Gothic Quarter, is a bustling world of shops, bars, and nightlife packed between otherwise uninteresting 14th- and 15th-century buildings. The section near the port is generally dull and seedy. But the area around the cathedral is a tangled-yet-inviting grab bag of undiscovered courtyards, grand squares, schoolyards, Art Nouveau storefronts, baby flea markets (on Thursdays), musty junk shops, classy antiques shops (on Carrer de la Palla), street musicians strumming Catalan folk songs, and balconies with domestic jungles behind wrought-iron bars. Go on a cultural scavenger hunt. Write a poem. This self-guided walk gives you a structure, covering the main sights and offering a historical overview before you get lost.

• *Start on Barcelona's bustling main square.*

Plaça de Catalunya: This square is the center of the world for seven million Catalan people. The square is decorated with the likenesses of important Catalans. From here, walls that contained the city until the 19th century arc around in each direction to the sea. Looking at your map of Barcelona, you'll see a regimented waffle design—except for the higgledy-piggledy old town corralled by these walls.

The city grew with its history. Originally a Roman town, Barcelona was ruled by the Visigoths from the fall of Rome until 714, when the Moors arrived (they were, in turn, sent packing by the French in 801—because their stay was cut so short, there are few Moorish-style buildings here). Finally, in the 10th century, the Count of Barcelona unified the region, and the idea of Catalunya came to be. The area between Plaça de Catalunya and the old Roman walls (circling the smaller ancient town, down by the cathedral) was settled by churches, each a magnet gathering a small

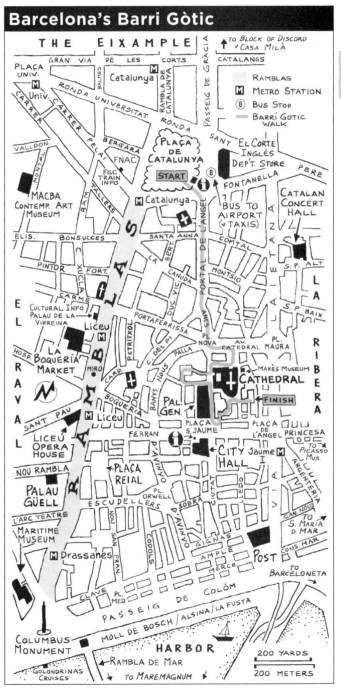

Barcelona's Barri Gòtic

community outside the walls (or "extra muro"). Around 1250, when these "extra muro" communities became numerous and strong enough, the king agreed to invest in a larger wall, and Barcelona expanded. This outer wall was torn down in the 1850s and replaced by a series of circular boulevards (named Rondas).

• *From Plaça de Catalunya's TI, head downhill, crossing the busy street (Calle Fontanella) into a broad pedestrian boulevard called...*

Avinguda Portal de l'Angel: This boulevard is named "Gate of the Angel" for the gate in the medieval wall—crowned by an angel—that once stood here. The angel kept the city safe from plagues and bid voyagers safe journey as they left the security of the city. Imagine the fascinating scene here at the Gate of the Angel, where Barcelona stopped and the wilds began.

While walking down the Avinguda Portal de l'Angel, consider an optional detour a half-block right on **Carrer de Santa Anna,** where a lane on the right leads into a courtyard facing one of those "extra muro" churches, with a fine cloister and simple, typically Romanesque facade.

Continuing down the main boulevard (Avinguda Portal de l'Angel), you reach a fork in the road with a blue-and-yellow-tiled **fountain.** This was once a freestanding well—in the 17th century, it was the last watering stop for horses before leaving town. Take the left fork to the cathedral (past the Architects' House, with its Picasso-inspired frieze).

Enter the square, where you'll stand before two bold **towers**—the remains of the old Roman wall that protected a smaller Barcino, as the city was called in ancient times. The big stones that make up the base of the towers are actually Roman. The wall stretches left of the towers, incorporated into the Deacon's House, which you'll enter from the other side later).

• *The sights from here on are located on the map on page 30. Walk around—past the modern bronze letters* BARCINO *and the mighty facade of the cathedral (which we'll enter momentarily)—and go inside the...*

Deacon's House (Casa de l'Ardiaca): Visitors are welcome inside this mansion, which today functions as the city archives (its front door faces the wall of the church). It's free to enter and a good example of a Renaissance nobleman's palace. Notice how the century-old palm tree seems to be held captive by urban man. Inside you can see the Roman stones up close. Upstairs affords a view of the cathedral's exterior—textbook Catalan Gothic (plain and practical, like this merchant community) next to textbook Romanesque (the smaller, once freestanding, more humble church adjacent on the right, which you'll visit entering from its cloister later).

• *Exit the house to the left and follow the lane. You'll emerge at the entrance to the...*

Cathedral of Barcelona (Catedral de Barcelona): This huge house of worship is worth a look. Its vast size, peaceful cloister, and many ornate chapels—each one sponsored by a local guild—are impressive. For a self-guided tour, see the "Cathedral of Barcelona" listing on page 29.

• *After visiting the cathedral's cloister, exit and walk to the tiny lane ahead on the right (far side of the statue, Carrer de Montjuïc del Bisbe). This leads to the cute...*

Plaça Sant Felip Neri: This square serves as the playground of an elementary school bursting with youthful energy. The Church of Sant Felip Neri, which Gaudí attended, is still pocked with bomb damage from the Civil War. As a stronghold of democratic, anti-Franco forces, Barcelona saw a lot of fighting. The shrapnel that damaged this church was meant for the nearby Catalan government building (Palau de la Generalitat, described below).

Study the medallions on the wall. Guilds powered the local economy, and the carved reliefs here show that this building must have housed the shoemakers. In fact, on this square you'll find a fun little Shoe Museum.

• *Circle the block back to the cathedral's cloister and take a right, walking along Carrer del Bisbe next to the huge building (on the right), which stretches all the way to the next square.*

Palau de la Generalitat: For more than 600 years, this place has been the home of the Catalan government. Through good times and bad, the Catalan spirit has survived, and this building has housed its capital.

• *Continue along Carrer del Bisbe to...*

Plaça de Sant Jaume (jow-mah): This stately central square of the Barri Gòtic, once the Roman forum, has been the seat of city government for 2,000 years. Today the two top governmental buildings in Catalunya face each other: the Barcelona City Hall (Ajuntament; free but only open to the public Sun 10:00–13:30) and the seat of the autonomous government of Catalunya (Palau de la Generalitat, described above). It always flies the Catalan flag (red and yellow stripes) next to the obligatory Spanish one. From these balconies, the nation's leaders (and soccer heroes) greet the people on momentous days.

• *Take two quick left turns from the corner of Carrer Bisbe (just 10 yards away), and climb Carrer del Paridís. Follow this street as it turns right, but pause when it swings left, at the summit of...*

"Mont" Tàber: A millstone in the corner marks ancient Barcino's highest elevation, a high spot in the road called Mount Tàber. A plaque on the wall says it all: "Mont Tàber, 16.9 meters." Step into the courtyard for a peek at a surviving corner of the imposing **Roman temple** (Temple Roma d'August) that once stood here on Mont Tàber, keeping a protective watch over Barcino (free, well-explained on wall in English, daily 10:00–14:00 & 16:00–20:00).

• *Continue down Carrer del Paridís back to the cathedral, take a right, and go downhill about 100 yards to...*

Plaça del Rei: The Royal Palace sat on this "King's Square" (a block from the cathedral) until Catalunya became part of Spain in the 15th century. Then it was the headquarters of the local Inquisition. In 1493, a triumphant Christopher Columbus, accompanied by six New World natives (whom he called "Indians") and several pure-gold statues, entered the Royal Palace. King Ferdinand and Queen Isabel rose to welcome him home, and they honored him with the title "Admiral of the Oceans."

• *Your tour is over. Nearby, just off Plaça del Rei, is the City History Museum. The Frederic Marès Museum is just up the street (toward the cathedral entrance; both described later). Or simply wander and enjoy Barcelona at its Gothic best.*

Sights in Barcelona

Barcelona's Old City

I've divided Barcelona's Old City sights into three neighborhoods: near the harbor, at the bottom of the Ramblas; the cathedral and nearby (Barri Gòtic); and the Picasso Museum and nearby (La Ribera).

On the Harborfront, at the Bottom of the Ramblas

▲**Maritime Museum (Museu Marítim)**—Barcelona's medieval shipyard, the best preserved in the entire Mediterranean, has an impressive collection covering the salty history of ships and navigation from the 13th to the 20th centuries. Riveting for nautical types, and interesting for anyone, its modern and beautifully presented exhibits will put you in a seafaring mood. The museum is

undergoing a major renovation, closing off large sections one at a time through 2013, so what you see will depend on when you visit. The museum's cavernous halls evoke the 14th-century days when Catalunya was a naval and shipbuilding power, cranking out 30 huge galleys a winter. As in the US today, military and commercial ventures mixed and mingled as Catalunya built its trading empire. The excellent included audioguide tells the story and explains the various seafaring vessels displayed—including an impressively huge and richly decorated royal galley (€2.50, prices may change as more exhibits reopen, daily 10:00–20:00, last entry at 19:30, breezy courtyard café, Avinguda de la Drassanes, tel. 933-429-920, www .mmb.cat).

▲**Columbus Monument (Monument a Colóm)**—Marking the point where the Ramblas hits the harbor, this 200-foot-tall monument built for an 1888 exposition offers an elevator-assisted view from its top. The tight four-person elevator takes you to the glassed-in observation area at the top for congested but sweeping views (€3, daily May–Oct 9:00–20:30, Nov–April 10:00–18:30). It was here in Barcelona that Ferdinand and Isabel welcomed Columbus home after his first trip to America. It's ironic that Barcelona would so honor the man whose discoveries ultimately led to its downfall as a great trading power.

Golondrinas **Cruises**—At the harbor near the foot of the Columbus Monument, tourist boats called *golondrinas* offer two different unguided trips. The shorter version goes around the harbor in 35 minutes (€6.50, daily on the hour 11:30–19:00, every 30 minutes mid-June–mid-Sept, may not run Nov–April—call ahead, tel. 934-423-106). The longer 1.5-hour trip goes up the coast to the Fòrum complex and back (€13.50, can disembark at Fòrum in summer only, about 7/day, daily 11:30–19:30, shorter hours in winter).

▲Cathedral of Barcelona

Most of the construction on Barcelona's vast cathedral (Catedral de Barcelona) took place in the 14th century, during the glory days of the Catalan nation. The facade was humble, so in the 19th century the proud local bourgeoisie redid it in a more ornate Neo-Gothic style.

BARCELONA

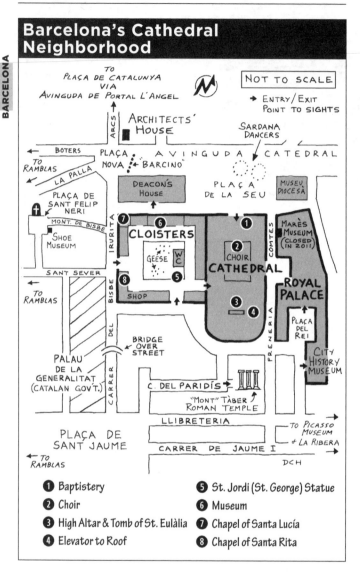

Barcelona's Cathedral Neighborhood

NOT TO SCALE

→ ENTRY/EXIT POINT TO SIGHTS

- ① Baptistery
- ② Choir
- ③ High Altar & Tomb of St. Eulàlia
- ④ Elevator to Roof
- ⑤ St. Jordi (St. George) Statue
- ⑥ Museum
- ⑦ Chapel of Santa Lucía
- ⑧ Chapel of Santa Rita

Cost and Hours: Strangely, even though the cathedral is free to enter daily 8:00–12:45 (until 13:45 on Sun) and 17:15–19:30, you must pay €5 to enter between 12:45 and 17:15 (tel. 933-151-554). The dress code is strictly enforced; don't wear tank tops, short shorts, or short skirts.

Getting There: The huge can't-miss-it cathedral is in the center of the Barri Gòtic, on Plaça de la Seu. For an interesting way to reach the cathedral from Plaça de Catalunya, and some commen-

tary on the surrounding neighborhood, see my self...
the Barri Gòtic, described earlier.

➲ Self-Guided Tour: Though the cathedra...
and supported by buttresses, it has smooth outside w...

because the supporting buttresses are on
the inside, providing walls for 28 richly
ornamented chapels. This, along with
the interior's open and spacious feeling, is characteristic of Catalan Gothic.
Typical of all medieval churches, the
cathedral has an "ambulatory" plan,
allowing worshippers to amble around
to the chapel of their choice.

Although the main part of the
church is fairly plain, the **chapels,** sponsored by local guilds, show great wealth.
Located in the community's most high-
profile space, they provided a kind of advertising to illiterate worshippers. The Native Americans that Columbus brought to town
were supposedly **baptized** in the first chapel on the left.

The chapels ring a finely carved 15th-century **choir** *(coro)*. For
€2.20 (no charge if you paid church entry fee), you can enter and
get a close-up look (with the lights on) of the ornately carved stalls
and the emblems representing the various Knights of the Golden
Fleece who once sat here. The chairs were folded up, giving VIPs
stools to lean on during the standing parts of the Mass. Each was
creatively carved and—since you couldn't sit on sacred things—the
artists were free to enjoy some secular and naughty fun here. Study
the upper tier of carvings.

The **high altar** sits upon the **tomb** of Barcelona's patron saint,
Eulàlia. She was a 13-year-old local girl tortured 13 times by
Romans for her faith before finally being crucified on an X-shaped
cross. Her X symbol is carved on the pews. Climb down the stairs
for a close look at her exquisite marble sarcophagus. Many of the
sarcophagi in this church predate the present building.

You can ride the **elevator** to the roof for a view (€2.50, no

charge if you paid church entry fee,
Mon–Fri 10:30–18:00, Sat 10:00–12:00,
closed Sun, start from chapel left of high
altar).

Enter the **cloisters** (through arch,
right of high altar). Once inside, look
back at the arch, an impressive mix of
Romanesque and Gothic. Nearby, a tiny
statue of St. George slaying the dragon
stands in the garden. Jordi (George) is

Sardana Dances

Patriotic *sardana* dances are held at the cathedral (every Sun at 12:00, usually also Sat at 18:00). Locals of all ages seem to spontaneously appear. For some it's a highly symbolic, politically charged action representing Catalan unity—but for most it's just a fun chance to kick up their heels. Participants gather in circles after putting their things in the center—symbolic of community and sharing (and the ever-present risk of theft). All are welcome, even tourists cursed with two left feet.

Holding hands, dancers raise their arms—slow-motion, *Zorba the Greek*-style—as they hop and sway gracefully to the music. The band *(cobla)* consists of a long flute, tenor and soprano oboes, strange-looking brass instruments, and a tiny bongo-like drum *(tambori)*. The rest of Spain mocks this lazy circle dance, but considering what it takes for a culture to survive within another culture's country, it is a stirring display of local pride and patriotism. The event lasts between one and two hours.

one of the patron saints of Catalunya and by far the most popular boy's name here. Cloisters are generally found in monasteries, but this church has one because it needed to accommodate more chapels—to make more money. With so many wealthy merchants in town who believed that their financial generosity would impress God and win them favor, the church needed more private chapel space. Merchants wanted to be buried close to the altar, and their tombs also spill over into the cloister. Notice on the pavement stones, as in the chapels, the symbols of the trades or guilds: scissors, shoes, bakers, and so on.

Long ago the resident **geese**—there are always 13, in memory of Eulàlia—functioned as an alarm system. Any commotion would get them honking, alerting the monk in charge. They honk to this very day.

From the statue of St. Jordi, circle to the right (past a WC hidden on the left). The skippable little €2 **museum** (far corner; no charge if you paid church entry fee) is one plush room with a dozen old religious paintings. Just beyond the museum, in the corner, built into the outside wall of the cloister, is the dark, barrel-vaulted Romanesque **Chapel of Santa Lucía,** a small church that predates the cathedral. People hoping for good eyesight (Santa Lucía's specialty) leave candles outside. Farther along the cloister, the **Chapel**

of Santa Rita (her forte: impossible causes) usually has the most candles.

In the Barri Gòtic, near the Cathedral

For an interesting route from Plaça de Catalunya to the cathedral neighborhood, see my self-guided walk of the Barri Gòtic. And if you're in town on a weekend, don't miss the *sardana* dances (see sidebar).

Shoe Museum (Museu del Calçat)—Shoe-lovers enjoy this two-room shoe museum, watched over by an earnest attendant. The huge shoes at the entry are designed to fit the foot of the Columbus Monument at the bottom of the Ramblas (€2.50, Tue–Sun 11:00–14:00, closed Mon, one block beyond outside door of cathedral cloister, behind Plaça de G. Bachs on Plaça Sant Felip Neri, tel. 933-014-533).

▲▲City History Museum (Museu d'Història de la Ciutat)— Walk through the history of the city with the help of an included audioguide. First watch the nine-minute introductory video in the small theater (playing alternately in Catalan, Spanish, and English)—it's worth viewing in any language. Then take an elevator down 65 feet (and 2,000 years—see the date spin back while you descend) to stroll the streets of Roman Barcelona. You'll see sewers, models of domestic life, and bits of an early-Christian church. Finally, an exhibit in the 11th-century count's palace shows you Barcelona through the Middle Ages (€7, free all day first Sun of month and other Sun from 15:00 in summer; Tue–Sat April–Sept 10:00–20:00, Oct–March 10:00–14:00 & 16:00–19:00, Sun 10:00–20:00, last entry 30 minutes before closing, closed Mon; Plaça del Rei, enter on Vageur street, tel. 932-562-122).

Frederic Marès Museum (Museu Frederic Marès)—This museum, which has been closed for renovation, may reopen by the summer of 2011. When open, its eclectic collection of local artist (and packrat) Frederic Marès sprawls around a peaceful courtyard through several old Barri Gòtic buildings. The biggest part of the collection is sculpture, hailing from ancient times to the early 20th century. But even more interesting is Marès' vast collection of items he found representative of everyday life in the 19th century—rooms upon rooms of fans, stamps, pipes, and other bric-a-brac, all lovingly displayed. There are also several sculptures by Frederic Marès himself, and temporary exhibits (closed for part of 2011; when it reopens, €4.20 admission may change, but hours and free days will stay the same: free Wed and Sun from 15:00; open Tue–Sat 10:00–19:00, Sun 10:00–20:00, closed Mon; Plaça de Sant Iu 5–6, tel. 932-563-500, www.museumares.bcn.cat). The delightfully tranquil courtyard café offers a nice break, even when the museum is closed.

BARCELONA

▲▲▲Picasso Museum (Museu Picasso)

This is the best collection in the country of the work of Spaniard Pablo Picasso (1881–1973), and—since he spent his formative years (age 14–21) in Barcelona—it's the best collection of his early works anywhere. By seeing his youthful, realistic art, you can more fully appreciate the artist's genius and better understand his later, more challenging art. The collection is scattered through several connected Gothic palaces, six blocks from the cathedral in the Ribera district.

Cost and Hours: €9, free all day first Sun of month and other Sun from 15:00, open Tue–Sun 10:00–20:00, closed Mon, Montcada 15–23, ticket office at #21, Metro: Jaume I, tel. 932-563-000, www.museupicasso.bcn.cat. The ground floor has a required bag check, as well as a handy array of other services (bookshop, WC, and cafeteria).

Crowd-Beating Tips: There's almost always a line, but it moves quickly (you'll rarely wait more than an hour to get in). The busiest time is from when it opens until about 13:00 (worst on Tuesdays), as well as on free days; generally the later in the afternoon you visit, the fewer the crowds. If you have an Articket Card, skip the line by going to the group entrance.

Eating: The museum itself has a good **café**. Nearby, the **Textil Café,** hiding in a beautiful and inviting museum courtyard across the street, is a decent place to sip a *café con leche* or eat a light meal (Tue–Sun 12:00–24:00, closed Mon, 30 yards from Picasso Museum at Montcada 12–14, tel. 932-954-657; also hosts jazz concerts Sunday nights 20:30–23:00, weather permitting—usually not in winter, no cover, but you have to order something). And just down the street is a neighborhood favorite for tapas, the recommended **El Xampanyet** (closed Mon).

Background: Picasso's personal secretary amassed a huge collection of his work and bequeathed it to the city. Picasso, happy to have a museum showing off his work in the city of his youth, added to the collection throughout his life. (Sadly, since Picasso vowed never to set foot in a fascist, Franco-ruled Spain, and died two years before Franco, the artist never saw the museum.)

❸ Self-Guided Tour: Though the rooms are sometimes rearranged, the collection (291 paintings) is always presented chronologically. With the help of thoughtful English descriptions for each stage (and blue-shirted guards who don't let you stray), it's easy to follow the evolution of Picasso's work. The room numbers—though not exact—can help you get oriented in the museum. You'll see his art evolve in these stages:

Room 1—Boy Wonder, Age 12–14: Pablo's earliest art is realistic and serious. A budding genius emerges at age 12, as Pablo moves to Barcelona and gets serious about art. Even this young, his portraits of grizzled peasants show great psychological insight and flawless technique. You'll see portraits of Pablo's first teacher, his father *(El Padre del Artista).* Displays show his art-school work. Every time Pablo starts breaking rules, he's sent back to the standard classic style. The assignment: Sketch nude models to capture human anatomy accurately. Early self-portraits (1896, 1897) show the self-awareness of a blossoming intellect (and a kid who must have been a handful in junior high school). When Pablo was 13, his father quit painting to nurture his young prodigy. Look closely at the portrait of his mother *(Retrato de la Madre del Artista).* Pablo, then age 15, is working on the fine details and gradients of white in her blouse and the expression in her cameo-like face. Notice the signature. Spaniards keep both parents' surnames, with the father's first, followed by the mother's: Pablo Ruiz Picasso. Pablo was closer to his mom than his dad, and eventually he kept just her name.

Room 2—Adolescence, Developing Talent: During a short trip to Málaga, Picasso dabbles in Impressionism (otherwise unknown in Spain at the time). As a 15-year-old, Pablo dutifully enters art-school competitions. His first big work—while forced to show a religious subject *(Primera Comunión,* or *First Communion)*—is more an excuse to paint his family. Notice his sister Lola's exquisitely painted veil. This piece was heavily influenced by local painters.

Room 3—Early Success: *Ciencia y Caridad (Science and Charity),* which won second prize at a fine-arts exhibition, got Picasso the chance to study in Madrid. Now Picasso conveys real feeling. The doctor (Pablo's father) represents science. The nun represents charity and religion. From her hopeless face and lifeless hand, it seems that Picasso believes nothing will save this woman from death. Pablo painted a little perspective trick: Walk back and forth across the room to see the bed stretch and shrink. Three small studies for this painting, hanging in the back of the room, show how this was an exploratory work. The frontier: light.

Picasso travels to Madrid for further study. Finding the stuffy fine-arts school in Madrid stifling, Pablo hangs out in the Prado Museum and learns by copying the masters. Notice his nearly perfect copy of Philip IV by Diego Velázquez. Having absorbed the wisdom of the ages, in 1898 Pablo visits Horta de San Juan, a rural Catalan village, and finds his artistic independence. Poor and without a love in his life, he returns to Barcelona.

Room 4—Barcelona Freedom, 1900: Art Nouveau is all the rage. Upsetting his dad, Pablo quits art school and falls in with the avant-garde crowd. These bohemians congregate daily at Els Quatre Gats ("The Four Cats," slang for "a few crazy people"—a popular restaurant to this day). Further establishing his artistic freedom, he paints portraits—no longer of his family...but of his new friends. Still a teenager, Pablo puts on his first one-man show.

Rooms 5–7—Paris, 1900–1901: Nineteen-year-old Picasso arrives in Paris, a city bursting with life, light, and love. Dropping the paternal surname Ruiz, Pablo establishes his commercial brand name: "Picasso." Here the explorer Picasso goes bohemian and befriends poets, prostitutes, and artists. He paints Impressionist landscapes like Claude Monet, cancan dancers like Toulouse-Lautrec, still lifes like Paul Cézanne, and bright-colored Fauvist works like Henri Matisse. (*La Espera*—with her bold outline and strong gaze—pops out from the Impressionistic background.) It was Cézanne's technique of "building" a figure with "cubes" of paint that inspired Picasso to invent Cubism soon.

Temporary Exhibits: As if to cleanse the museumgoer's palate before plunging into the major works, you'll now walk through some temporary exhibits.

Room 8—Blue Period, 1901–1904: The bleak Paris weather, the suicide of his best friend, and his own poverty lead Picasso to his "Blue Period." He cranks out piles of blue art just to stay housed and fed. With blue backgrounds (the coldest color) and depressing subjects, this period was revolutionary in art history. Now the artist is painting not what he sees but what he feels. The touching portrait of a mother and child, *Desamparados* (*Despair*, 1903), captures the period well. Painting misfits and street people, Picasso, like Velázquez and Toulouse-Lautrec, sees "the beauty in ugliness." Back home in Barcelona, Picasso paints his hometown at night from rooftops *(Azoteas de Barcelona)*. The paintings still blue, here we see proto-Cubism...five years before the first real Cubist painting.

Room 9—Rose Period, 1904–1907: The woman in pink *(Retrato de la Señora Canals)*, painted with classic "Spanish melancholy," finally lifts Picasso out of his funk, moving him out of the blue and into a happier "Rose Period" (of which this museum has only the one painting).

Room 11—Cubism, 1907–1920: Pablo's invention in Paris of the shocking Cubist style is well-known—at least I hope so, since this museum has no true Cubist paintings. In the age of the camera, the Cubist gives just the basics (a man with a bowl of fruit) and lets you finish it. (In the museum you'll see some so-called "Synthetic Cubist" paintings—a later variation that flattens the various angles, as opposed to the purer, original "Analytical Cubist" paintings, in which you can simultaneously see several 3-D facets of the subject.)

Also in Rooms 9 and 10—Eclectic, 1920–1950: Picasso is a painter of many styles. In *Mujer con Mantilla* (Room 9), we see a little Post-Impressionistic Pointillism in a portrait that looks like a classical statue. After a trip to Rome, he paints beefy women, inspired by the three-dimensional sturdiness of ancient statues. To Spaniards, the expressionist horse symbolizes the innocent victim (Room 10). In bullfights, the horse—clad with blinders and pummeled by the bull—has nothing to do with the fight. To Picasso, the horse symbolizes the feminine, and the bull, the masculine. Picasso mixes all these styles and symbols—including this image of the horse—in his masterpiece *Guernica* (in Madrid's Centro de Arte Reina Sofía) to show the horror and chaos of modern war.

• *From here, backtrack through rooms 8–11, and follow signs for* Ending/Collection *to Rooms 12–14.*

Rooms 12–14—Picasso and Velázquez, 1957: Notice the small print of Velázquez's *Las Meninas* (the original is displayed in Madrid's Prado). Picasso, who had great respect for Velázquez,

painted more than 50 interpretations of this piece that many consider the greatest painting by anyone, ever. These two Spanish geniuses were artistic equals. Picasso seems to enjoy a relationship with Velázquez. Like artistic soul mates, they spar and tease. He dissects Velázquez, and then injects playful uses of light, color, and perspective to horse around with the earlier masterpiece. In the big black-and-white canvas, the king and queen (reflected in the mirror in the back of the room) are hardly seen, while the self-portrait of the painter towers above everyone. The two women of the court on the right look like they're in a tomb—but they're wearing party shoes. In these rooms, see the fun Picasso had playing paddleball with Velázquez's masterpiece—filtering Velázquez's realism through the kaleidoscope of Cubism.

Picasso said many times that "Paintings are like windows open to the world." In Room 14, we see the French Riviera—with simple black outlines and Crayola colors, Picasso paints sun-splashed nature and the joys of the beach. He died with brush in hand, still growing. To the end, Picasso continued exploring and loving life through his art. As a child, he was taught to paint as an adult. Now, as an old man (with little kids of his own and also-childlike artist Marc Chagall for a friend), he paints like a child.

Barcelona's La Ribera

- ❶ Gothic Point Hostel
- ❷ Sagardi Euskal Taberna Rest. & Bar
- ❸ Taller de Tapas
- ❹ El Xampanyet Bar
- ❺ Textil Café
- ❻ 1714 Massacre Monument
- ❼ Un Cotxe Menys Bike Rental

Rooms 15–16—Ceramics, 1947: As a wrap-up, walk through this room with 41 ceramic works Picasso made during his later years.

In La Ribera, near the Picasso Museum

There's more to the Ribera neighborhood than just the Picasso Museum. While the nearby waterfront Barceloneta district was for the working-class sailors, La Ribera housed the wealthier shippers and merchants. Its streets are lined with their grand mansions—

which, like the much-appreciated Church of Santa Maria del Mar, were built with shipping wealth.

La Ribera (also known as "El Born") is separated from the Barri Gòtic by Via Laietana, a four-lane highway built through the Old City in the early 1900s to alleviate growing traffic problems. From the Plaça de l'Angel (nearest Metro stop—Jaume I), cross this busy street to enter an up-and-coming zone of lively and creative restaurants and nightlife. The Carrer de l'Argenteria ("Goldsmiths Street"—streets in La Ribera are named after the workshops that used to occupy them) runs diagonally from the Plaça de l'Angel straight down to the Church of Santa Maria del Mar. The Catalan Concert Hall is to the north.

▲▲Catalan Concert Hall (Palau de la Música Catalana)—This concert hall, finished in 1908, features my favorite Modernista interior in town (by Lluís Domènech i Muntaner). Inviting arches lead you into the 2,138-seat hall. A kaleidoscopic skylight features a choir singing around the sun, while playful carvings and mosaics celebrate music and Catalan culture. You can only get in by tour, which starts with a relaxing 12-minute video (€12, 50-minute tours in English run daily every hour 10:00–15:00, may have longer hours on weekends and holidays, tour times may change based on performance schedule, about 6 blocks northeast of cathedral, tel. 932-957-200, www.palaumusica.org).

The Catch: You must buy your ticket in advance to get a spot on an English guided tour (tickets available up to 7 days in advance—ideally buy yours at least 2 days before, though they're sometimes available the same day or day before). You can buy the ticket in person at the concert hall box office (open daily 9:30–15:30); by phone with your credit card (toll tel. 902-485-475); or online at the concert hall website (€1 fee, www.palaumusica.org).

It might be easier to get tickets for a **concert** (300 per year, tickets for some performances as cheap as €7, see website for details).

▲Church of Santa Maria del Mar—This church is the proud centerpiece of La Ribera. "Del Mar" means "of the sea," and that's where the money came from. The proud shippers built this

church in only 55 years, so it has a harmonious style that is considered pure Catalan Gothic. As you step in, notice the figures of workers carved into the big front doors. During the Spanish Civil War (1936–1939), the Church sided with the conservative forces of Franco against the people. In retaliation, the working class took their anger out on this church, burning all of its wood furnishings and decor (carbon still blackens the ceiling). Today it's stripped down—naked in all its Gothic glory. The tree-like columns inspired Gaudí (their influence on the columns inside his Sagrada Família church is obvious). Sixteenth-century sailors left models of their ships at the foot of the altar for Mary's protection. Even today there remains a classic old Catalan ship at Mary's feet. As within Barcelona's cathedral, here you can see the characteristic Catalan Gothic buttresses flying inward, defining the chapels that ring the nave (free entry, daily 9:00–13:30 & 16:30–20:00).

Exit the church from the side, and you arrive at a square with a modern **monument** to a 300-year-old massacre that's still part of the Catalan consciousness. On September 11, 1714, the Bourbon king ruling from Madrid massacred Catalan patriots, who were buried in a mass grave on this square. From that day on, the king outlawed Catalan culture and its institutions (no speaking the language, no folk dances, no university, and so on). The eternal flame burns atop this monument, and 9/11 is still a sobering anniversary for the Catalans.

To the Picasso Museum: From behind the church, the Carrer de Montcada leads two blocks to the Picasso Museum (described earlier). The street's mansions—built by rich shippers centuries ago—now house galleries, shops, and even museums. The Picasso Museum itself consists of five such mansions laced together.

Passeig del Born—Just behind the church, this long square was formerly a jousting square (as its shape indicates). This is the neighborhood center and a popular springboard for exploring tapas bars, fun restaurants, and nightspots in the narrow streets all around. Wandering around here at night, you'll find piles of inviting and intriguing little restaurants. Enjoy a glass of wine on the square facing the church, or consider renting a bike here for a pedal down the beach promenade to the Fòrum (described on next page).

Chocolate Museum (Museu de la Xocolata)—This museum, only a couple of blocks from the Picasso Museum (and near Citadel Park—see next), is a delight for chocolate-lovers. Operated by the local confectioners' guild, it tells the story of chocolate from Aztecs to Europeans via the port of Barcelona, where it was first unloaded and processed. But the history lesson is just an excuse to show off a series of remarkably ornate candy sculptures. These works of edible art—which change every year but often include such Spanish themes as Don Quixote or bullfighting—begin as store-window displays for Easter or Christmas. Once the holiday passes, the confectioners bring the sculptures here to be enjoyed (€4.30, Mon and Wed–Sat

10:00–19:00, Sun 10:00–15:00, closed Tue, Carrer Comerç 36, tel. 932-687-878, www.museuxocolata.com).

Near the Waterfront, East of the Old City and Harbor

Citadel Park (Parc de la Ciutadella)—In 1888 Barcelona's biggest, greenest park, originally the site of a much-hated military citadel, was transformed for a World's Fair (Universal Exhibition). The stately Triumphal Arch at the top of the park, celebrating the removal of the citadel, was built as the main entrance. Inside you'll find wide pathways, plenty of trees and grass, a zoo, and museums of geology and zoology. Barcelona, one of Europe's most densely populated cities, suffers from a lack of real green space. This park is a haven, and is especially enjoyable on weekends, when it teems with happy families. Enjoy the ornamental fountain that the young Antoni Gaudí helped design, and consider a jaunt in a rental rowboat on the lake in the center of the park. Check out the tropical Umbracle greenhouse and the Hivernacle winter garden, which has a pleasant café-bar (daily 8:00–20:00, Metro: Arc de Triomf, east of França train station).

▲**Barcelona's Beach, from Barceloneta to the Fòrum**— Barcelona has created a summer tourist beach trade by building

a huge stretch of beaches east from the town center. Before the 1992 Olympics, this area was an industrial wasteland nicknamed the "Catalan Manchester." Not anymore. The industrial zone was demolished and dumped into the sea, while sand was dredged out of the sea bed to make the pristine beaches locals enjoy today. The scene is great for sunbathing and for an evening paseo before dinner. It's like a resort island— complete with lounge chairs, volleyball, showers, bars, WCs, and bike paths.

Bike the Beach: For a break from the city, rent a bike (in La Ribera or Citadel Park) and take the following little ride: Explore Barcelona's "Central Park"—Citadel Park—filled with families enjoying a day out (described above). Then roll through Barceloneta. This artificial peninsula was once the home of working-class sailors and shippers. From the Barceloneta beach, head west to the Olympic Village, where the former apartments for 13,000 visiting athletes now house permanent residents. The village's symbol, Frank Gehry's striking "fish," shines brightly in the sun. A bustling night scene keeps this stretch of harborfront busy until the wee hours. From here you'll come to a series of man-made crescent-shaped beaches, each with trendy bars and cafés. If you're careless or curious (down by Platja de la Mar Bella), you might find yourself pedaling through people working on an all-over tan. In the distance you see the huge solar panel marking the site of the Fòrum shopping and convention center.

The Fòrum—The original 1860 vision for Barcelona's enlargement continued the boulevard called Diagonal right to the sea. Developers finally realized this goal nearly a century and a half later, with the opening of the Fòrum. Go here for a taste of today's Barcelona: nothing Gothic, nothing quaint, just big and modern—a mall and a convention center. In 2004 Barcelona hosted the "Forum of the Cultures," an attempt to create a world's fair that recognized not states, but peoples. Roma (Gypsies), Basques, Māoris, Native Americans, and Catalans all assembled here in a global celebration of cultural diversity, multiculturalism, peace, and sustainability.

The Fòrum also tries to be an inspiration for environmental engineering. Waste is burned to create heat. The giant solar panel creates perfectly clean and sustainable energy. The bash for this planet's "nations without states" was a moderate success, with follow-ups in Mexico in 2007 and Chile in 2010. Local government officials hoped the event—like other "expos"—would goose development...and it did. Barcelona now has a modern part of town.

You can get out to the Fòrum by bike, bus, or taxi via the long and impressive beach. Or the Metro zips you there in just a few minutes from the center (L4/yellow line, Fòrum Station). Once there, browse around the modern shopping zone.

The Eixample: Modernisme and Antoni Gaudí

Wide sidewalks, hardy shade trees, chic shops, and plenty of Art Nouveau fun make the Eixample a refreshing break from the Old City. For the best Eixample example, ramble Rambla de Catalunya (unrelated to the more famous Ramblas) and pass through Passeig de Gràcia (Metro for Block of Discord: Passeig de Gràcia, or Metro for Casa Milà: Diagonal).

The 19th century was a boom time for Barcelona. By 1850 the city was busting out of its medieval walls. A new town was planned to follow a grid-like layout. The intersection of three major thoroughfares—Gran Via, Diagonal, and Meridiana—would shift the city's focus uptown. But uptown Barcelona is a unique variation on the common grid-plan city: Barcelona snipped off the building corners to create light and spacious eight-sided squares at every intersection.

The Eixample, or "Expansion," was a progressive plan in which everything was made accessible to everyone. Each 20-block-square district would have its own hospital and large park, each 10-block-

Modernisme

The Renaixensa (Catalan cultural revival) gave birth to Modernisme (Catalan Art Nouveau) at the end of the 19th century. Barcelona is its capi-tal. Its Eixample neighborhood shimmers with the colorful, leafy, flowing, blooming shapes of Modernisme in doorways, entrances, facades, and ceilings. Meaning "a taste for what is modern"—things like streetcars, electric lights, and big-wheeled bicycles—this free-flowing organic style lasted from 1888 to 1906. Breaking with tradition, artists experimented with glass, tile, iron, and brick. The structure was fully modern, using rebar and concrete, but the decoration was a clip-art collage of nature images, exotic Moorish or Chinese themes, and fanciful Gothic crosses and knights to celebrate Catalunya's medieval glory days. It's Barcelona's unique contribution to the Europe-wide Art Nouveau movement. Modernisme was a way of life as Barcelona burst into the 20th century.

Antoni Gaudí (1852–1926), Barcelona's most famous Modernista artist, was descended from four generations of metalworkers, a lineage of which he was quite proud. He incorporated ironwork into his architecture and came up with novel approaches to architectural structure and space.

Two more Modernista architects famous for their unique style are Lluís Domènech i Muntaner and Josep Puig i Cadafalch. You'll see their work on the Block of Discord.

square area would have its own market and general services, and each five-block-square grid would house its own schools and day-care centers. The hollow space found inside each "block" of apartments would form a neighborhood park.

Although much of that vision never quite panned out, the Eixample was an urban success. Rich and artsy big shots bought plots along the grid. The richest landowners built as close to the center as possible. For this reason, the best buildings are near the Passeig de Gràcia. While adhering to the height, width, and depth limitations, they built as they pleased—often in the trendy new Modernista style.

For many visitors, Modernista architecture is Barcelona's main draw. (The TI even has a special desk set aside just for Modernisme-seekers.) And one name tops them all: **Antoni Gaudí** (1852–1926). Barcelona is an architectural scrapbook of Gaudí's galloping gables and organic curves. A devoted Catalan and Catholic, he immersed himself in each project, often living on-site. At various times, he called Parc Güell, Casa Milà, and the Sagrada Família home.

First I've covered the main Gaudí attractions close to the Old City. The Sagrada Família and Parc Güell are farther afield, but worth the trip. And since many visitors do those two sights together, I've included tips on how to connect them.

Gaudí Sights near the Old City

▲▲**Casa Milà (La Pedrera)**—This Gaudí exterior laughs down on the crowds filling Passeig de Gràcia. Casa Milà, also called La Pedrera ("The Quarry"), has a much-photographed roller coaster of melting-ice-cream eaves. This is Barcelona's quintessential Modernista building and was Gaudí's last major work (1906–1910) before dedicating his final years to the Sagrada Família.

You can visit three sections of Casa Milà: the apartment, the attic, and the rooftop (€10, good audioguide-€3, daily March–Oct 9:00–20:00, Nov–Feb 9:00–18:30, last entry 30 minutes before closing, Passeig de Gràcia 92, Metro: Diagonal, toll tel. 902-400-973). If you pay for an audioguide, you can choose between the 1.25-hour tour, which offers more listening options, or the 30-minute version.

After entering, head upstairs. Two elevators take you up to either the apartment or the attic. Normally you're directed to the apartment, but if you arrive late in the day, go to the attic elevator first, then climb right up to the rooftop to make sure you have enough time to enjoy Gaudí's works and the views.

The typical fourth-floor **apartment** is decorated as it might have been when the building was first occupied by middle-class

urbanites (a seven-minute video explains Barcelona society at the time). Notice Gaudí's clever use of the atrium to maximize daylight in all of the apartments.

The **attic** houses a sprawling multimedia "Gaudí Space," tracing the history of the architect's career with models, photos, and videos of his work. It's all displayed under distinctive parabola-shaped arches. While evocative of Gaudí's style in themselves, the arches are formed this way partly to sup-

Visit Casa Milà or Casa Batlló?

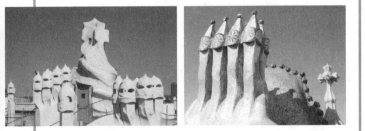

These two Antoni Gaudí houses offer similar, up-close looks at Modernista architecture. Casa Batlló's rooftop (above right) is smaller, all on one level, and less impressive than the expansive rooftop at Casa Milà (above left). But the unfurnished Casa Batlló is less of a museum and better allows the architecture to speak for itself. If you're choosing one, Casa Milà is cheaper and has the superior rooftop, but Gaudí fans will find both worthwhile.

port the multilevel roof above. This area was also used for ventilation, helping to keep things cool in summer and warm in winter. Tenants had storage spaces and did their laundry up here.

From the attic, a stairway leads to the fanciful, undulating, jaw-dropping **rooftop,** where 30 chimneys play volleyball with the clouds.

Back at the **ground level** of Casa Milà, poke into the dreamily painted original entrance courtyard. The first floor hosts free art exhibits.

Concerts: During July, a rooftop concert series called "Pedrera by Night" features live music—jazz, flamenco, tango—and gives you the chance to see the rooftop illuminated (around €13, 22:00–24:00, toll tel. 902-400-973, http://obrasocial.caixacatalunya.es).

Eating: Stop by the recommended **La Bodegueta,** a long block away (daily lunch special).

▲**Block of Discord**—Four blocks from Casa Milà, you can survey a noisy block of competing late-19th-century facades. Several of Barcelona's top Modernista mansions line Passeig de Gràcia (Metro: Passeig de Gràcia). Because the structures look as though they are trying to outdo each other in creative twists, locals nicknamed the block between Consell de Cent and Arago the "Block of Discord."

First (at #43) and most famous is Gaudí's **Casa Batlló,** with skull-like balconies and a tile roof that suggests a cresting dragon's

Modernista Sights

ⓑ Bus Stop Ⓜ Metro Station

RONDA DE DALT

TORRE DE BELLESGUARD

FINCA GÜELL

FINCA MIRALLES

COL·LEGI DE LAS TERESIANES

GIRONA

DIAGONAL

SANTS TRAIN STN.

TRAV. GRACIA

LESSEPS

CASA VICENS

ⓑ #24

FONTANA

GAUDÍ HOUSE + MUSEUM

PARC GÜELL

#24, #92 + TOURIST BUS

TERRACE + FRONT ENTRANCE

TRAV. DALT

HOSPITAL DE LA SANTA CREU I SANT PAU (BY MUNTANER)

BLOCK OF DISCORD

- CASA BATLLÓ BY GAUDÍ
- CASA AMATLLER BY CADAFALCH
- CASA LLEÓ MORERA BY MUNTANER

DIAGONAL

CASA MILÀ

ⓑ #92

PROVENÇA

ⓑ #19 + #50

SAGRADA FAMÍLIA

PASSEIG DE GRÀCIA

GRAN VIA

PLAÇA D'ESPANYA

PARAL·LEL

PLAÇA DE CATALUNYA + ⓑ #24

CASA CALVET

CATALAN CONCERT HALL (BY MUNTANER)

MONTJUÏC

LICEU Ⓜ

RAMBLAS

BARRI GÒTIC

PALAU GÜELL

DRASS.

FRANÇA TRAIN STN.

OLYMPIC PORT + "FISH" (BY GEHRY)

NOT TO SCALE

DCH

HARBOR

---

back; Gaudí based the work on the popular legend of St. Jordi (George) slaying the dragon. You can tour the house—a rival of Casa Milà (described earlier) (€17.80, includes audioguide, daily 9:00–20:00, may close early for special events—closings posted in advance at entrance, tel. 932-160-306, www.casabatllo .cat). You'll see the main floor (with a funky mushroom-shaped fireplace nook), the blue-and-white-ceramic-slathered atrium, the attic (more parabolic arches), and the rooftop, all with the help of the good audioguide. Because preservation of the place is privately funded, the entrance fee is steep—but the interior is even more fanciful and over-the-top than Casa Milà's. There's barely a straight line in

the house. By the way, if you're tempted to snap photos from the middle of the street, be careful—Gaudí died under a streetcar.

Next door, at **Casa Amatller** (#41), check out architect Josep Puig i Cadafalch's creative mix of Moorish- and Gothic-inspired architecture and iron grillwork, which decorates a step-gable like those in the Netherlands. Pop inside for a peek at the elaborate entrance hall.

On the corner (at #35), **Casa Lleó Morera** has a wonderful interior highlighted by the dining room's fabulous stained glass. The architect, Lluís Domènech i Muntaner, also designed the Catalan Concert Hall (you'll notice similarities).

The recommended **La Rita** restaurant, just around the corner on Carrer Arago, serves a fine three-course lunch for a great price (Mon–Fri from 13:00).

▲**Palau Güell**—Just as the Picasso Museum reveals a young genius on the verge of a breakthrough, this early Gaudí building (completed in 1890) shows the architect taking his first tentative steps toward what would become his trademark curvy style. The parabolic-arch doorways, viewable from the outside, are the first clue that this is not a typical townhouse. In the midst of an extensive renovation, only part of the house is open to the public: the main floor and the Neo-Gothic cellar (which was used as a stable—notice the big carriage doors in the back and the rings on some of the posts used to tie up the horses). By 2011, they hope to have more of the house open...and start charging admission (free, Tue–Sat 10:00–14:30, closed Sun–Mon, a half-block off the Ramblas at Carrer Nou de la Rambla 3–5, tel. 933-173-974, www.palauguell.cat). Even if the rooftop—with its fanciful mosaic chimneys (visible from the street if you crane your neck)—is open, I'd skip it if you plan to see the more interesting one at Casa Milà.

▲▲▲Sagrada Família (Holy Family Church)

Gaudí's most famous and persistent work is this unfinished landmark church. He worked on the Sagrada Família from 1883 until his death in 1926. Since then, construction has moved forward in fits and starts. Even today, the half-finished church is not expected

to be completed for another quarter-century. (But over 30 years of visits, I've seen considerable progress.) The temple is funded exclusively by private donations and entry fees, which is another reason its completion has taken so long. Your admission helps pay for the ongoing construction.

Cost and Hours: €12, daily April–Sept 9:00–20:00, Oct–March

9:00–18:00, Metro: Sagrada Família puts you right on the door-step—exit toward *Pl de la Sagrada Família*, tel. 932-073-031, www.sagradafamilia.cat.

Crowd-Beating Tips: The ticket line can be very long (up to about 30–45 minutes at peak times). In summer, it's generally least crowded during lunch and after 18:30, and most crowded right when the church opens. To skip the ticket-buying line, purchase tickets in advance online (www.servicaixa.com, pick up at ServiCaixa terminal outside the Passion Facade) or at any ServiCaixa machine (located throughout the city).

Tours: The 45-minute English tours cost €4 (May–Oct daily at 11:00 and 13:00, Nov–April usually Fri–Mon only, same times). Or rent the good 70-minute audioguide (also €4).

Elevators: Two different elevators take you partway up the towers for a great view of the city and a gargoyle's-eye perspective of the loopy church. Each one costs €2.50 (pay as you board elevator). The **Passion facade elevator** takes you 215 feet up, where you can climb higher if you want; then an elevator takes you back down. The **Nativity facade elevator** is similar, but you can also cross the dizzying bridge between the towers—and you must walk all the way down. (Some people prefer the Nativity elevator despite the additional steps because it offers close views of the facade that Gaudí actually worked on.) For the climbing sections, expect the spiral stairs to be tight, hot, and congested. Lines for both elevators can be very long (up to a 2-hour wait at the busiest times); signs along the stanchions give you an estimated wait time. To avoid long lines, follow the "Crowd-Beating Tips" (above) and go directly to the elevators when you arrive. The Nativity facade elevator generally has a shorter line.

The Construction Project: There's something powerful about an opportunity to feel a community of committed people with a vision, working on a church that will not be finished in their lifetime (as was standard in the Gothic age). Local craftsmen often cap off their careers by spending a couple of years on this exciting construction site. The church will trumpet its completion with 18 spires: A dozen "smaller" 330-foot spires (representing the apostles) will stand in groups of four and mark the three entry facades of the building. Four taller towers (dedicated to the four Evangelists) will surround the two tallest, central towers: a 400-foot-tall tower of Mary and the grand 550-foot Jesus tower, which will shine like a spiritual lighthouse—visible even from out at sea. A unique exterior ambulatory will circle the building, like a cloister turned inside out. If there's any building on earth I'd like to see, it's the Sagrada Família...finished.

❍ Self-Guided Tour: To get a good rundown, follow this commentary.

• *Begin by facing the western side of the church (where you'll enter).*

Passion Facade: It seems strange to begin with something that Gaudí had nothing to do with...but that's where they put the entrance. When Gaudí died in 1926, only the stubs of four spires stood above the building site. The rest of the church has been inspired by Gaudí's vision but designed and executed by others. Gaudí knew he wouldn't live to complete the church and recognized that later architects and artists would rely on their own muses for inspiration. This artistic freedom was amplified in 1936, when Civil War shelling burned many of Gaudí's blueprints. Judge for yourself how the recently completed and controversial Passion facade by Josep María Subirachs (b. 1927) fits with Gaudí's original formulation (which you'll see downstairs in the museum).

Subirachs' facade is full of symbolism from the Bible. The story of Christ's Passion unfolds in the shape of a Z, from bottom to top. Find the stylized Alpha and Omega over the door; Jesus—hanging on the cross—with an open book (the word of God) for hair; and the grid of numbers adding up to 33 (Jesus' age at the time of his death). The distinct face of the man below and just left of Christ is a memorial to Gaudí.

Now look high above: The figure perched on the bridge between the towers is the soul of Jesus, ascending to heaven. The colorful ceramic caps of the towers symbolize the miters (formal hats) of bishops.

Grand and impressive as this seems, keep in mind it's only the *side* entry to the church. The nine-story apartment building to the right will be torn down to accommodate the grand front entry. The three facades—Passion, Nativity, and Glory—will chronicle Christ's life from birth to death to resurrection.

• *We'll enter the church later. For now, look right to find the...*

School: Gaudí erected this school for the children of the workers building the church. Now it houses an exhibit focusing on the architect's use of geometric forms. You'll also see a classroom and a replica of Gaudí's desk as it was the day he died, and a model for the proposed Glory facade...the next big step.

• *Leaving the school, turn right and go down the ramp under the church, into the...*

Museum: Housed in what is someday intended to be the church's crypt, the museum runs underground from the Passion facade to the Nativity facade. The first section tells the chronological story of the Sagrada Família. Look for the replicas of the pulpit and confessional that Gaudí, the micro-manager, designed for his church. As you wander through the plaster models used for the church's construction, you'll notice that they don't always match the finished product—these are ideas, not blueprints set in stone. Photos show the construction work as it was when Gaudí died in 1926 and how it's progressed over the years. See how the church's design is a fusion of nature, architecture, and religion. The columns seem light, with branches springing forth and capitals that look like palm trees.

Walking down the long passage to the other side of the church, you'll pass under a giant plaster model of the nave (you'll see the real thing soon). Find the hanging model showing how Gaudí used gravity to calculate the perfect parabolas incorporated into the church design (the mirror above this model shows how the right-side-up church is derived from this). Nearby, you'll find some original Gaudí architectural sketches in a dimly lit room and a worthwhile 20-minute movie (generally shown in English at :50 past each hour).

Then you'll peek into a busy workshop for making plaster models of the planned construction, just like what Gaudí used—he found these helpful for envisioning the final product in 3-D. The museum wraps up with an exhibit on the design and implementation of the Passion facade.

• *Climb up the ramp and hook left to see the…*

Nativity Facade (east side): This, the only part of the church essentially finished in his lifetime, shows Gaudí's original vision. (Cleverly, this facade was built and finished first to inspire financial support, which Gaudí knew would be a challenge.) Mixing Gothic-style symbolism, images from nature, and Modernista asymmetry, it is the best example of Gaudí's unmistakable cake-in-the-rain style. The sculpture shows a unique twist on the Nativity, with Jesus as a young carpenter and angels playing musical instruments.

• *From here you have two options:*

To take the elevator up the Nativity facade, go through the small door to the right of the main door. The line stretches through an area called the Rosary Cloister.

To enter the church (where you'll also find the Passion facade elevator entrance), go in the door to the left of the main entry. First you'll pass the Montserrat Cloister, with the **Gaudí and Nature** *exhibition that compares nature, waves, shells, mushrooms, the ripple of a leaf, and so on to Gaudí's work. Then you'll enter the…*

Construction Zone (the Nave): The cranking cranes, rusty forests of rebar, and scaffolding require a powerful faith, but the Sagrada Família offers a fun look at a living, growing bigger-than-life building. Part of Gaudí's religious vision was a love for

nature. He said, "Nothing is invented; it's written in nature." His columns blossom with life, and little windows let light filter in like the canopy of a rain forest, giving both privacy and an intimate connection with God. The U-shaped choir hovers above the nave, tethered halfway up the columns. A relatively recent addition—hanging out in the middle of the back wall—is a statue of Barcelona's patron saint, St. Jordi (George of dragon-slaying fame). The nave's roof was just completed in 2010. At the far end of the nave, you'll see the line to take the elevator up the Passion facade.

Finishing the floors in the nave was a priority before Pope Benedict XVI's visit on November 7, 2010, to consecrate of the church. Currently, the construction is focused on a few major tasks: stabilizing the existing nave (which has been rattled by vibrations from the Metro and AVE train lines underground) and eventually adding the third, biggest entry—the Glory facade. They're also in the process of replacing the temporary clear windows with stained-glass ones. The final phase is the central tower (550 feet tall), which, it's estimated, will require four underground support pylons, each consisting of 8,000 tons of cement.

Gaudí lived on the site for more than a decade, and is buried in a Neo-Gothic 19th-century crypt (which is where the church began). His tomb is viewable for free from the small church around the corner from the main ticket entrance (during Mass—Mon–Sat 8:30–10:00 & 18:30–21:00, longer hours on Sun). There's a move afoot to make Gaudí a saint. Perhaps someday his tomb will be a place of pilgrimage. Gaudí—a faithful Catholic whose medieval-style mysticism belied his Modernista architecture career—was certainly driven to greatness by his passion for God. When undertaking a lengthy project, he said, "My client"—meaning God—"is in no hurry."

Scenic Connection to Parc Güell: If your next stop is Parc Güell (described next), and you don't want to spring for a taxi, try this route: With the Nativity facade at your back, walk to the near-left corner of the park across the street. Then cross the street to reach the diagonal Avinguda Gaudí (between the Repsol gas station and the KFC). From here you'll follow the funky lampposts four blocks gradually uphill (about 10 minutes) along Avinguda Gaudí, a pleasantly shaded, café-lined pedestrian street. When you reach the striking Modernista-style Hospital de la Santa Creu i Sant Pau (designed by Lluís Domènech i Muntaner), cross the street and go up one block (left) on St. Antonio Maria Claret street to catch bus #92, which will take you to the side entrance of Parc Güell.

From the Sagrada Família, you could also get to Parc Güell by taking the Metro to Lesseps, then bus #24 (described under "Getting There" for Parc Güell), but that involves two changes... and less scenery.

More Bus Connections: From the Sagrada Família, bus #19 makes an easy 15-minute journey to the Old City (stops near the cathedral and La Ribera district); bus #50 goes from the Sagrada Família, to the corner of Gran Via de les Corts Catalanes and Passeig de Gràcia, and to Montjuïc, skipping the funicular but taking you past all the sights.

▲Parc Güell

Gaudí fans enjoy the artist's magic in this colorful park. Gaudí intended this 30-acre garden to be a 60-residence housing proj-

ect—a kind of gated community. As a high-income housing development, it flopped; but as a park, it's a delight, offering another peek into Gaudí's eccentric genius. Notice the mosaic medallions that say "park" in English, reminding folks that this is modeled on an English garden.

Cost and Hours: Free, daily 10:00–20:00, tel. 932-130-488.

Getting There: From Plaça de Catalunya, the red Tourist Bus or bus #24 will leave you at the park's side entrance, or a €8 taxi will drop you off at the main entrance. From elsewhere in the city, do a Metro-plus-bus combination: Go by Metro to the Lesseps stop. To avoid the tiring uphill 20-minute walk to the park, don't follow the *Parc Güell 1300 metros* sign; instead, exit the Metro station, cross the streets Princep d'Astúries and Gran de Gràcia, and catch bus #24 (on Gran de Gràcia), which takes you to the park's side entrance in less than 10 minutes.

◐ Self-Guided Tour: This tour assumes you're arriving at the front/main entrance (by taxi). If you're instead arriving by bus at the side entrance, walk straight ahead through the gate to find the terrace with colorful mosaic benches, then walk down to the stairway and front entrance.

As you wander the park, imagine living here a century ago—if this gated community had succeeded and was filled with Barcelona's wealthy.

Front Entrance: Entering the park, you walk by Gaudí's wrought-iron gas lamps (1900–1914). His dad was a blacksmith, and he always enjoyed this medium. Two gate houses made of gingerbread flank the entrance. One houses a good bookshop; the other is home to the skippable Center for Interpretation of Parc Güell (Centre d'Interpretació), which shows Gaudí's building methods plus maps, photos, and models of the park (€2.30, daily 11:00–15:00, tel. 933-190-222). The Gaudí House and Museum, described later, is better.

Stairway and Columns: Climb the grand stairway, past the famous ceramic dragon fountain. At the top, dip into the "Hall of 100 Columns," designed to house a produce market for the neighborhood's 60 mansions. The fun columns—each different, made from concrete

and rebar, topped with colorful ceramic, and studded with broken bottles and bric-a-brac—add to the market's vitality.

As you continue up (on the left-hand staircase), look left, down the playful "pathway of columns" that supports a long arcade. Gaudí drew his inspiration from nature, and this arcade is like a surfer's perfect tube.

Terrace: Once up top, sit on a colorful bench—designed to fit your body ergonomically—and enjoy one of Barcelona's best views. Look for the Sagrada Família church in the distance. Gaudí was an engineer as well. He designed a water-catchment system by which rain hitting this plaza would flow into and through the columns from the market below, and power the park's fountains.

When considering the failure of Parc Güell as a community development, also consider that it was an idea a hundred years ahead of its time. Back then, high-society ladies didn't want to live so far from the cultural action. Today, the surrounding neighborhoods are some of the wealthiest in town, and a gated community here would be a big hit.

Gaudí House and Museum: This pink house with a steeple, standing in the middle of the park (near the side entrance), was actually Gaudí's home for 20 years, until his father died. His humble artifacts are mostly gone, but the house is now a museum with some quirky Gaudí furniture and a chance to wander through a model home used to sell the others. Though small, it offers a good taste of what could have been (€5.50, daily April–Sept 10:00–20:00, Oct–March 10:00–18:00).

Montjuïc

Montjuïc ("Mount of the Jews"), overlooking Barcelona's hazy port, has always been a show-off. Ages ago it had an impressive fortress. In 1929 it hosted an international fair, from which most of today's sights originated. And in 1992 the Summer Olympics directed the world's attention to this pincushion of attractions once again.

I've listed these sights by altitude, from highest to lowest; if you're visiting all of them, do them in this order so that most of your walking is downhill (for selective sightseers, the Fundació Joan Miró and Catalan Art Museum are the most worthwhile). Note that if you want to visit only the Catalan Art Museum, you can just take the Metro to Plaça d'Espanya and ride the escalators up (with some stair-climbing as well) to the museum.

Getting to Montjuïc: You have several options. The simplest is to take a **taxi** directly to your destination (about €7 from downtown).

Buses from various points in the city take you up to Montjuïc, including public bus #50 (from the corner of Gran Via and Passeig de Gràcia, or from the Sagrada Família), public bus #55 (from Plaça de Catalunya, next to Caja de Madrid building), and the blue Tourist Bus.

A **funicular** takes visitors from the Paral-lel Metro stop up to Montjuïc (covered by a Metro ticket, every 10 minutes, 9:00–22:00). To reach the funicular, take the **Metro** to the Paral-lel stop, then follow signs for *Parc Montjuïc* and the little funicular icon—you can enter the funicular directly without using another ticket (number of minutes until next departure posted at start of entry tunnel). From the top of the funicular, turn left and walk two minutes to the Joan Miró museum, six minutes to the Olympic Stadium, or ten minutes to the Catalan Art Museum.

From the port, the most scenic way to Montjuïc is on the **cable car,** called the 1929 Transbordador Aereo (€9 one-way, €12.50 round-trip, 3/hour, daily 10:45–19:00, until 20:00 in June–Sept, closed in high wind, tel. 932-252-718).

Getting Around Montjuïc: Up top, the bus marked *Parc de Montjuïc* (#PM) loops between the sights. This circular line starts at Plaça d'Espanya and goes to the Catalan Art Museum, the Joan Miró museum, the funicular, and the Castle of Montjuïc. Public bus #50 and

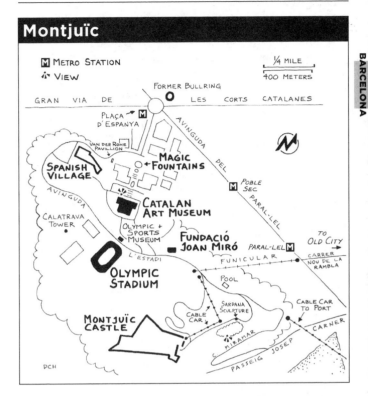

Montjuïc

M METRO STATION
↟ VIEW

¼ MILE
400 METERS

FORMER BULLRING

GRAN VIA DE O LES CORTS CATALANES

PLAÇA → M
D'ESPANYA

AVINGUDA DEL

VAN DER ROHE
PAVILLION

SPANISH
VILLAGE

MAGIC ←FOUNTAINS

POBLE
SEC M

AVINGUDA

CATALAN
ART MUSEUM

CALATRAVA
TOWER

OLYMPIC ↟
SPORTS
MUSEUM

FUNDACIÓ
JOAN MIRÓ

PARAL-LEL M

TO
OLD CITY →

L'ESTADI

FUNICULAR

CARRER
NOU DE LA
RAMBLA

OLYMPIC
STADIUM

CABLE
CAR ↓

POOL

SARDANA
SCULPTURE

CABLE CAR
TO PORT

MONTJUÏC
CASTLE

MIRAMAR

CARNER

C

PASSEIG JOSEP

DCH

the blue Tourist Bus also do circuits around the top of Montjuïc.

Castle of Montjuïc—The castle offers great city views from its fortress. The castle itself has a fascist past rife with repression. It was built in the 18th century by the central Spanish government to keep an eye on Barcelona and stifle citizen revolt. When Franco was in power, the castle was the site of hundreds of political executions (free, daily April–Sept 9:00–21:00, Oct–March 9:00–19:00, tel. 932-564-445, www.bcn.cat/castelldemontjuic).

Getting There: To spare yourself the hike up to the castle, and to catch some great views of the city, take the **cable car** from just above the upper station of the Montjuïc funicular (€6.30 one-way, €9 round-trip, June–Sept daily 10:00–21:00, until 19:00 April–May and Oct, until 18:00 Nov–March).

▲**Fundació Joan Miró**—Showcasing the talents of yet another Catalan artist, this museum has the best collection of Joan Miró art anywhere. You'll also see works by other Modern artists (such as *Mercury Fountain* by American sculptor Alexander Calder). If you don't like abstract art, you'll leave here scratching your head. But those who love this place are not faking it...they understand the genius of Miró and the fun of abstract art.

As you wander, consider this: Miró believed that everything in the cosmos is linked—colors, sky, stars, love, time, music, dogs, men, women, dirt, and the void. He mixed childlike symbols of these things creatively, as a poet uses words. It's as liberating for the visual artist to be abstract as it is for

the poet: Both can use metaphors rather than being confined to concrete explanations. Miró would listen to music and paint. It's interactive, free interpretation. He said, "For me, simplicity is freedom."

Here are some tips to help you enjoy and appreciate Miró's art: first meditate on it, then read the title (for example, *The Smile of a Tear*), then meditate on it again. Repeat the process until you have an epiphany. There's no correct answer—it's pure poetry. Devotees of Miró say they fly with him and don't even need drugs. You're definitely much less likely to need drugs if you take advantage of the wonderful audioguide, well worth the €4 extra charge (€8.50, Tue–Sat July–Sept 10:00–20:00, Oct–June 10:00–19:00, Thu until 21:30, Sun 10:00–14:30, closed Mon, 200 yards from top of funicular, Parc de Montjuïc,

COPA DEL MUNDO DE FUTBOL ESPAÑA 82

tel. 934-439-470, www.bcn.fjmiro.es). The museum has a cafeteria, a café, and a bookshop.

Olympic and Sports Museum (Museu Olímpic i de l'Esport)—This museum, opened in 2007, rides the coattails of the stadium across the street (see next listing). You'll twist down a timeline-ramp that traces the history of the Olympic Games, interspersed with random exhibits about various sports. Downstairs you'll find exhibits designed to test your athleticism, a play-by-play rehash of the '92 Barcelona Olympiad, a commemoration of Spaniard Juan Antonio Samaranch (the influential president of the IOC for two decades), a sports media exhibit, and a schmaltzy movie collage. High-tech but hokey, the museum is worth the time and money only for those nostalgic for the '92 Games (€4, Tue–Sat April–Sept 10:00–20:00, Oct–March 10:00–18:00, Sun 10:00–14:30, closed Mon, Avinguda de l'Estadi 60, tel. 932-925-379, www.fundaciobarcelonaolimpica.es).

Olympic Stadium (Estadi Olímpic)—For two weeks in the

summer of 1992, the world turned its attention to this stadium (between the Catalan Art Museum and the Fundació Joan Miró at Passeig Olímpic 17). Redesigned from an earlier 1929 version, the stadium was updated, expanded, and officially named for Catalan patriot Lluís Companys i Jover. The XXV Olympiad kicked off here on July 25, when an archer dramatically lit the Olympic torch—which still stands high at the end of the stadium overlooking the city skyline—with a flaming arrow. Over the next two weeks, Barcelona played host to the thrill of victory (most memorably at the hands of Michael Jordan, Magic Johnson, Larry Bird, and the rest of the US basketball "Dream Team") and the agony of defeat (i.e., the nightmares of the Dream Team's opponents). Hovering over the stadium is the futuristic Montjuïc Communications Tower, designed by Santiago Calatrava and used to transmit Olympic highlights and lowlights around the world. Aside from the memories of the medals, Olympic Stadium offers little to see today...except when it's hosting a match for Barcelona's soccer team, RCD Espanyol.

Spanish Village (Poble Espanyol)—This tacky five-acre model village uses fake traditional architecture from all over Spain as a shell to contain gift shops. Craftspeople do their clichéd thing only in the morning (not worth your time or €8.90, www.poble -espanyol.com). After hours, it's a popular local nightspot.

▲▲Catalan Art Museum (Museu Nacional d'Art de Catalunya)—The big vision for this wonderful museum is to showcase Catalan art from the 10th century through about 1930. Often called "the Prado of Romanesque art" (and "MNAC" for short),

it holds Europe's best collection of Romanesque frescoes (€8.50, ticket valid for two days within one month, includes audioguide, free first Sun of month, open Tue–Sat 10:00–19:00, Sun 10:00–14:30, closed Mon, last entry 30 minutes before closing; in massive National Palace building above Magic Fountains, near Plaça d'Espanya—take escalators up; tel. 936-220-376, www.mnac.es).

As you enter, pick up a map (helpful for such a big and confusing building). The left wing is Romanesque, and the right wing is Gothic, exquisite Renaissance, and Baroque. Upstairs is more Baroque, plus modern art, photography, coins, and more.

The MNAC's rare, world-class collection of **Romanesque** art came mostly from remote Catalan village churches in the Pyrenees (saved from unscrupulous art dealers, including many Americans). The Romanesque wing features frescoes, painted wooden altar fronts, and ornate statuary. This classic Romanesque art—with flat 2-D scenes, each saint holding his symbol, and Jesus (easy to identify by the cross in his halo)—is impressively displayed on replicas of the original church ceilings and apses.

Across the way, in the **Gothic** wing, fresco murals give way to vivid 14th-century wood-panel paintings of Bible stories. A roomful of paintings (Room 34) by the Catalan master Jaume Huguet (1412–1492) deserves a look, particularly his altarpiece of Barcelona's patron saint, George.

For a break, glide under the huge dome (which once housed an ice-skating rink) over to the air-conditioned cafeteria. This was the prime ceremony room and dance hall for the 1929 International Exposition. Then, from the big ballroom, ride the glass elevator upstairs, where the **Modern** section takes you on a delightful walk from the late 1800s to about 1930. It's kind of a Catalan Musée d'Orsay, offering a big chronological clockwise circle covering Spain's Golden Age (Zurbarán, heavy religious scenes, Spanish royals with their endearing underbites), Symbolism and Modernisme (furniture complements the empty spaces you likely saw in Gaudí's buildings), Impressionists, *fin de siècle* fun, and Art Deco.

Upstairs you'll also find photography (with a bit on how photojournalism came of age covering the Spanish Civil War), seductive sofas, and the chic Oleum restaurant, with vast city views (and €20 meals).

▲**Magic Fountains (Font Màgica)**—Music, colored lights, and huge amounts of water make an artistic and coordinated splash on summer nights at Plaça d'Espanya (20-minute shows start on the half-hour; almost always May–Sept Thu–Sun 21:00–23:30, no shows Mon–Wed; Oct–April Fri–Sat 19:00–21:00, no shows Sun–Thu; from the Espanya Metro station, walk toward the towering National Palace).

Away from the Center

Tibidabo—Tibidabo comes from the Latin for "to thee I shall give," the words the devil used when he was tempting Christ. It's still an enticing offer: At the top of Barcelona's highest peak, you're offered the city's oldest fun-fair (€25, erratic hours, tel. 932-117-942, www.tibidabo.es), the Neo-Gothic Sacred Heart Church, and—if the weather and air quality are good—an almost limitless view of the city and the Mediterranean.

Getting there is part of the fun: Start by taking the L7 Metro line from the Plaça de Catalunya Station (under Café Zürich) to the Tibidabo stop. (The red Tourist Bus stops here, too.) Then take Barcelona's only remaining tram—the Tramvía Blau—from Plaça John F. Kennedy to Plaça Dr. Andreu (€4.10 round-trip, 2–4/hour).

From there, take the funicular to the top (€4, fare is reimbursable with paid admission, tel. 906-427-017). A special "Tibibus" runs from Plaça de Catalunya to the park every day at 10:30 (€2.60, reimbursable with paid admission).

Nightlife in Barcelona

Refer to the *See Barcelona* guide (free from TI) and ask about the latest at a TI. Major sights open until 20:00 include the Picasso Museum (closed Mon), Gaudí's Sagrada Família (daily, until 18:00 Oct–March), Casa Milà (daily, until 18:30 Nov–Feb), and Parc Güell (daily). On Thursday, Montjuïc's Joan Miró museum stays open until 21:30 (otherwise open July–Sept Tue–Sat until 20:00).

Many lesser sights also stay open at least until 20:00, such as La Boquería market (Mon–Sat), Columbus Monument (May–Oct daily), City History Museum (April–Sept Tue–Sun), Church of Santa Maria del Mar (daily), Casa Batlló (daily), Parc Güell's Gaudí House and Museum (April–Sept daily), Castle of Montjuïc (April–Sept daily), and Citadel Park (daily). The Magic Fountains on Plaça d'Espanya make a splash on weekend evenings (Fri–Sat, plus Thu and Sun in summer). The Tourist Bus runs until 22:00 every day in summer.

Music and Entertainment: The weekly *Guía del Ocio,* sold at newsstands for €1 (or free in some hotel lobbies), is a Spanish-language entertainment listing (with guidelines for English-speakers inside the back cover; www.guiadelocio.com). The monthly *Barcelona Metropolitan* magazine and quarterly *What's On Barcelona* are also helpful (free from the TI). For music, consider a performance at Casa Milà ("Pedrera by Night" July concert series), the Liceu Opera House, or the Catalan Concert Hall. There are many nightspots around Plaça Reial (such as the popular Jamboree).

Palau de la Virreina, an arts-and-culture TI, offers information on Barcelona cultural events—music, opera, and theater (daily 10:00–20:00, Ramblas 99).

Sleeping in Barcelona

Book ahead. Barcelona is Spain's most expensive city. Still, it has reasonably priced rooms. Cheap places are more crowded in summer; fancier business-class hotels fill up in winter and offer discounts on weekends and in summer. When considering relative hotel values, in summer and on weekends you can often get modern comfort in business-class hotels for about the same price (€100) as you'll pay for ramshackle charm (and only a few minutes'

Sleep Code

(€1 = about $1.25, country code: 34)
S = Single, **D** = Double/Twin, **T** = Triple, **Q** = Quad, **b** = bathroom, **s** = shower only. Unless otherwise noted, credit cards are accepted, English is spoken, and prices listed generally include the 7-8 percent tax. Hotel breakfasts can range from free to simple €3 spreads to €25 buffets.

To help you easily sort through these listings, I've divided the rooms into three categories, based on the price for a standard double room with bath (during high season):

$$$ **Higher Priced**—Most rooms €150 or more.
 $$ **Moderately Priced**—Most rooms between €100-150.
  $ **Lower Priced**—Most rooms €100 or less.

Prices can change without notice; verify the hotel's current rates online or by email. For other updates, see www .ricksteves.com/update.

While many of my recommendations are on pedestrian streets, night noise can be a problem (especially in cheap places, which have single-pane windows). For a quiet night, ask for "*tranquilo*" rather than "*con vista.*"

---

walk from the Old City action). Some TI branches (including those at Plaça de Catalunya, Plaça de Sant Jaume, and the airport) offer a room-finding service, though it's cheaper to go direct. Note that prices at the Hotel Continental Barcelona and the Hotel Continental Palacete include great all-day snack-and-drink bars; several other hotels also offer free breakfasts to those who book direct with this guidebook.

Business-Class Comfort near Plaça de Catalunya

These hotels have sliding-glass doors leading to plush reception areas, air-conditioning, and perfectly sterile modern bedrooms. Most are on big streets within two blocks of Barcelona's exuberant central square. As business-class hotels, they have hard-to-pin-down prices that fluctuate wildly. I've listed the average rate you'll pay. But in summer and on weekends, supply often far exceeds the demand, and many of these places cut prices to around €100—always ask for a deal.

$$$ **Hotel Catalonia Duques de Bergara** has four stars, an elegant old entryway, splashy public spaces, slick marble and hardwood floors, 150 comfortable but simple rooms, and a garden courtyard with a pool a world away from the big-city noise (Db-€200 but can drop to as low as €100, extra bed-€35, breakfast-€16,

non-smoking rooms available on request, air-con, elevator, free Internet access and Wi-Fi, a half-block off Plaça de Catalunya at Carrer de Bergara 11, tel. 933-015-151, fax 933-173-442, www.hoteles-catalonia.com, duques@hoteles-catalonia.es).

$$$ Nouvel Hotel, in an elegant, Victorian-style building on a handy pedestrian street, is less business-oriented and offers more character than the others listed here. It boasts royal lounges and 78 comfy rooms (Sb-€110, Db-€192, includes breakfast; manager Roberto promises a 10 percent discount on these prices with this book in 2011—you must reserve direct by email, not their website; extra bed-€35, deposit for TV remote-€20, air-con, elevator, free Wi-Fi, Carrer de Santa Ana 20, tel. 933-018-274, fax 933-018-370, www.hotelnouvel.com, info@hotelnouvel.com).

$$ Hotel Reding, on a quiet street a five-minute walk west of the Ramblas and Plaça de Catalunya action, is a slick and sleek place renting 44 mod rooms at a good price (Db-€120—this rate includes breakfast with this book in 2011 but only if you book direct, prices go up during trade fairs, extra bed-€38, breakfast-€14, online deals don't include breakfast, non-smoking rooms, air-con, elevator, free Internet access and Wi-Fi, near Metro: Universitat, Gravina 5–7, tel. 934-121-097, fax 932-683-482, www.hotelreding.com, recepcion@hotelreding.com).

$$ Hotel Duc de la Victoria, with 156 rooms, is professional yet friendly, buried in the Barri Gòtic just three blocks off the Ramblas (Db-€140, bigger "superior" rooms on a corner with windows on 2 sides-€25 extra, breakfast-€15, non-smoking, air-con, elevator, Internet access, pay Wi-Fi, Duc 15, tel. 932-703-410, fax 934-127-747, www.nh-hotels.com, nhducdelavictoria@nh-hotels.com).

$$ Hotel Lleó (YEH-oh) is well-run, with 89 big, bright, and comfortable rooms; a great breakfast room; and a generous lounge (Db-€130 but flexes way up with demand, can be cheaper in summer, extra bed-about €30, breakfast-€13, non-smoking rooms, air-con, elevator, small rooftop pool, free Internet access and Wi-Fi, 2 blocks west of Plaça de Catalunya at Carrer de Pelai 22, tel. 933-181-312, fax 934-122-657, www.hotel-lleo.com, info@hotel-lleo.com).

$$ Hotel Atlantis is solid, with 50 big, homey-yet-mod rooms and great prices for the location (Sb-€90, Db-€107, Tb-€125, breakfast-€9, non-smoking rooms, air-con, elevator, free Internet access and Wi-Fi, older windows let in a bit more street noise than other hotels in this category—request a room with double-paned windows or a quieter room in back, Carrer de Pelai 20, tel. 933-189-012, fax 934-120-914, www.hotelatlantis-bcn.com, inf@hotelatlantis-bcn.com).

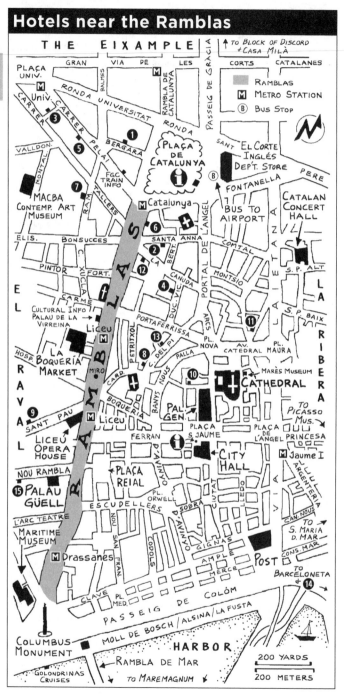

BARCELONA

Hotels Key

1. Hotel Catalonia Duques de Bergara
2. Nouvel Hotel
3. Hotel Reding
4. Hotel Duc de la Victoria
5. Hotels Lleó & Atlantis
6. Hotel Continental Barcelona
7. Hostería Grau & Barcelona Rent-A-Bike
8. Hotel Jardí
9. Hostal Opera
10. Hotel Neri
11. Hotel Regencia Colón
12. Hostal Campi
13. Hostal Maldá
14. To Sea Point Hostel
15. Launderette

Hotels with "Personality" on or near the Ramblas

These recommended places are generally family-run, with ad-lib furnishings, more character, and lower prices. Only the Jardí offers a quaint square buried in the Barri Gòtic ambience—but you're definitely paying for the location.

$ Hotel Continental Barcelona, in a building overlooking the top of the Ramblas, offers an inviting lounge and classic, tiny-view balcony opportunities if you don't mind the noise. Its comfortable rooms come with double-thick mattresses, wildly clashing carpets and wallpaper, and perhaps one too many clever ideas (they're laden with microwaves, fridges, a "command center" of light switches, and Tupperware drawers). Choose between your own little Ramblas-view balcony (where you can eat your breakfast) or a quieter back room (Sb-€90, Db-€100, twin Db-€110, Db with Ramblas balcony-€120, extra bed-€40, 5 percent discount with this book in 2011, prices include breakfast, non-smoking, air-con, elevator, free Internet access and Wi-Fi, Ramblas 138, tel. 933-012-570, fax 933-027-360, www.hotelcontinental.com, barcelona@hotelcontinental.com). J. M.'s (José María) free breakfast and all-day snack-and-drink bar make this a better deal than the price suggests.

$ Hostería Grau is homey, family-run, and almost alpine. Its 25 cheery, garden-pastel rooms are a few blocks off the Ramblas in the colorful university district. The first two floors have seven-foot-high ceilings, then things get tall again (S-€35, D-€65, Db-€90, extra bed-€15; 2-bedroom family suites: Db-€95, Tb-€130, Qb-€160; slippery prices jump during fairs and big events, prices include breakfast when you book direct and show this book in 2011, air-con, lots of stairs with no elevator, free Internet access and Wi-Fi, 200 yards up Carrer dels Tallers from the Ramblas at Ramelleres 27, tel. 933-018-135, fax 933-176-825, www.hostalgrau.com, reservas@hostalgrau.com, Monica). Before booking, confirm the hotel's strict cancellation policy—generally if canceling a room less than 48 hours in advance (or a suite less than five days in advance), you'll pay for the first night.

$ Hotel Jardí offers 40 clean, remodeled rooms on a breezy square in the Barri Gòtic. Many of the tight, plain, comfy rooms come with petite balconies (for an extra charge) and enjoy an almost Parisian ambience. It's a good deal only if you value the cute square location. Book well in advance, as this family-run place has an avid following (small basic interior Db-€70, nicer interior Db-€85, outer Db with balcony or twin with window-€90, large outer Db with balcony or square-view terrace-€100, add €5 to these rates on weekends, extra bed-€12, breakfast-€6, non-smoking, air-con, elevator, some stairs, free Wi-Fi in lobby, halfway between Ramblas and cathedral at Plaça Sant Josep Oriol 1, tel. 933-015-900, fax 933-425-733, www.hoteljardi-barcelona.com, reservations@hotel jardi-barcelona.com).

$ Hostal Opera, with 70 stark rooms 20 yards off the Ramblas, is clean, institutional, and modern. The street can feel seedy at night, but it's safe, and the hotel is very secure (Sb-€39–60, Db-€59–90, no breakfast, air-con only in summer, elevator, fee for Internet access and free Wi-Fi in lobby, Carrer Sant Pau 20, tel. 933-188-201, www.operaramblas.com, info@operaramblas.com).

Deep in the Barri Gòtic

$$$ Hotel Neri is chic, posh, and sophisticated, with 22 rooms spliced into the ancient stones of the Barri Gòtic, overlooking an overlooked square (Plaça Sant Felip Neri) a block from the cathedral. It has big plasma-screen TVs, pricey modern art on the bedroom walls, and dressed-up people in its gourmet restaurant (Db-€265, suites-€360–425, generally cheaper on weekdays, breakfast-€21, air-con, elevator, free Wi-Fi, rooftop tanning deck, St. Sever 5, tel. 933-040-655, fax 933-040-337, www.hotelneri .com, info@hotelneri.com).

$$ Hotel Regencia Colón, one block in front of the cathedral square, offers 50 solid, well-priced rooms in a handy location (Db-€105, more on weekends, breakfast-€12, air-con, elevator, Carrer Sagristans 13–17, tel. 933-189-858, fax 933-172-822, www .hotelregenciacolon.com, info@hotelregenciacolon.com).

Humble, Cheaper Places Buried in the Old City

$ Hostal Campi is big, subdued, and ramshackle, but offers simple class. This easygoing old-school spot rents 24 rooms a few doors off the top of the Ramblas (S-€33, D-€56, Db-€65, T-€75, Tb-€85, no breakfast, non-smoking rooms, lots of stairs with no eleva-

tor, pay Internet access, Canuda 4, tel. & fax 933-013-545, www
.hostalcampi.com, reservas@hostalcampi.com, friendly Margarita
and Nando).

$ Hostal Maldá rents the best cheap beds I've found in the
old center. With 25 rooms above a small shopping mall near the
cathedral, it's a time-warp—quiet and actually charming—but
does not take reservations (though you can try calling a day
before). It generally remains full through the summer, but it's
worth a shot (S-€15, D-€30, T-€45, cash only, lots of stairs with
no elevator, 100 yards up Carrer del Pi from delightful Plaça Sant
Josep Oriol, Carrer del Pi 5, tel. 933-173-002). Good-natured
Aurora doesn't speak English, but Delfi, who works only half the
year, does.

Hostels in the Center of Town

Barcelona has a wonderful chain of well-run and centrally located
hostels (www.equity-point.com), providing €21–26 dorm beds in
4- to 14-bed coed rooms with €2 sheets and towels, free Internet
access, Wi-Fi, breakfast, lockers (B.Y.O. lock, or buy one there),
and plenty of opportunities to meet other backpackers. They're
open 24 hours but aren't party hostels, so they enforce quiet after
23:00. There are three locations to choose from: Eixample, Barri
Gòtic, or near the beach.

$ Centric Point Hostel is a huge place renting 430 cheap
beds at what must be the best address in Barcelona (bar, kitchen,
Passeig de Gràcia 33, tel. 932-151-796, fax 932-461-552, www.cen-
tricpointhostel.com).

$ Gothic Point Hostel rents 150 beds a block from the
Picasso Museum (roof terrace, Carrer Vigatans 5, tel. 932-687-808,
www.gothicpoint.com).

$ Sea Point Hostel has 70 beds on the beach nearby (Plaça
del Mar 4, tel. 932-247-075, www.seapointhostel.com).

In the Eixample

For an uptown, boulevard-like neighborhood, sleep in the
Eixample, a 10-minute walk from the Ramblas action.

$$ Hotel Granvía, filling a palatial 1870s mansion, offers
Botticelli and chandeliers in the public areas; a sprawling, peaceful
sun patio; and 54 spacious, comfy rooms. Its salon is plush and
royal, making the hotel an excellent value for romantics. To reduce
street noise, ask for a quiet interior room or a room overlooking
the courtyard in the back of the building (Sb-€80, Db-€130 or
€110 July–Aug, Tb-€150, these rates promised with this book in
2011 when you reserve direct by phone or email—not on their
website—and mention my name, breakfast-€11, non-smoking, air-
con, elevator, free Internet access and Wi-Fi, Gran Via de les Corts

BARCELONA

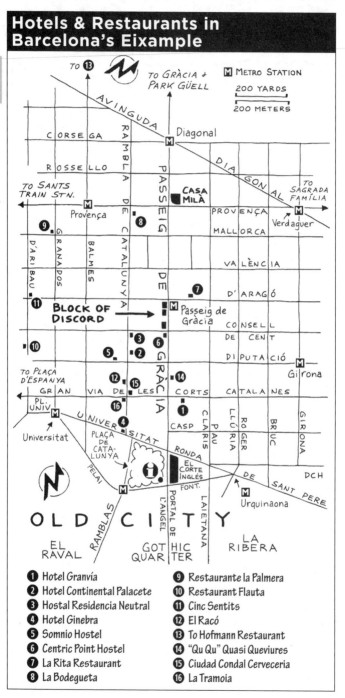

Hotels & Restaurants in Barcelona's Eixample

Ⓜ Metro Station

200 YARDS
200 METERS

TO ⑬
TO GRÀCIA +
PARK GÜELL

AVINGUDA

CORSEGA

Diagonal

ROSSELLO

RAMBLA DE CATALUNYA

PASSEIG DE CATALUNYA

DIAGONAL

TO SANTS
TRAIN STN.

CASA
MILÀ

PROVENÇA

Provença

TO
SAGRADA
FAMÍLIA

Verdaguer

⑨

⑧

MALLORCA

D'ARIBAU

GRANADOS

BALMES

VALÈNCIA

⑪

D'ARAGÓ

BLOCK OF
DISCORD

⑦

Passeig de
Gràcia

CONSELL

⑩

③ ⑥

⑤ ②

DE CENT

DIPUTACIÓ

Girona

TO PLAÇA
D'ESPANYA

⑫ ⑮

GRAN VIA DE

⑯

⑭

LESIA

CORTS

CATALANES

GRÀCIA

PL.
UNIV.

UNIVERSITAT

④

CASP

CLARIS

PAU

LLÚRIA

ROGER

BRUC

GIRONA

Universitat

PLAÇA
DE
CATALUNYA

RONDA

DE

SANT PERE

DCH

PELAI

EL
CORTE
INGLÉS
FONT.

ⓘ

Urquinaona

N

O L D   C I T Y

RAMBLAS

L'ANGEL

PORTAL DE

LAIETANA

EL
RAVAL

GOT
QUAR

HIC
TER

LA
RIBERA

❶ Hotel Granvía
❷ Hotel Continental Palacete
❸ Hostal Residencia Neutral
❹ Hotel Ginebra
❺ Somnio Hostel
❻ Centric Point Hostel
❼ La Rita Restaurant
❽ La Bodegueta

❾ Restaurante la Palmera
❿ Restaurant Flauta
⓫ Cinc Sentits
⓬ El Racó
⓭ To Hofmann Restaurant
⓮ "Qu Qu" Quasi Queviures
⓯ Ciudad Condal Cerveceria
⓰ La Tramoia

Catalanes 642, tel. 933-181-900, fax 933-189-997, www.hotelgran
via.com, hgranvia@nnhotels.com, Juan works the morning shift).

$$ Hotel Continental Palacete, with 19 rooms, fills a
100-year-old chandeliered mansion. With flowery wallpaper and
ornately gilded stucco, it's gaudy in the city of Gaudí, but it's
also friendly, clean, quiet, and well-located. Most of the rooms
are recently updated, there's an outdoor terrace, and guests have
unlimited access to the extravagant "cruise-inspired" fruit, veg-
gie, and drink buffet—worth factoring into your comparison-
shopping (Sb-€102, Db-€137, €35–45 more for bigger and brighter
view rooms, extra bed-€55, 5 percent discount with this book in
2011, prices include breakfast, non-smoking, air-con, free Internet
access and Wi-Fi, 2 blocks north of Plaça de Catalunya at corner
of Carrer Diputació, Rambla de Catalunya 30, tel. 934-457-657,
fax 934-450-050, www.hotelcontinental.com, palacete@hotel
continental.com).

$ Hostal Residencia Neutral, with a central Eixample
address and 28 very basic rooms, is a family-run time warp and a
fine value (tiny S-€38, Ds-€65, Db-€70, Ts-€80, Tb-€85, Qb-€89,
€6 continental breakfast in pleasant breakfast room, request a back
room to avoid street noise, thin walls, fans, elevator, free Internet
access and Wi-Fi, elegantly located 2 blocks north of Gran Via at
Rambla de Catalunya 42, tel. 934-876-390, fax 934-876-848, www
.hostalneutral.es, info@hostalneutral.es, Julia and Anna).

$ Hotel Ginebra is minimal, clean, and quiet considering
its central location. The Herrera family rents 12 rooms in a dated
apartment building overlooking the main square (Db-€75-80,
extra bed-€15, breakfast-€3, air-con, elevator, free Wi-Fi, Rambla
de Catalunya 1/3, tel. 933-171-063, www.hotelginebra.net, info
@hotelginebra.net, Juan speaks English).

$ Somnio Hostel, an innovative newer place run by a pair of
American expats, has both dorm beds and private rooms (dorm
bed-€25, S-€42, D-€77, Db-€85; prices include sheets, towels, and
lockers; air-con, elevator, free Internet access and Wi-Fi, Carrer
de la Diputació 251, second floor, tel. 932-725-308, www.somnio
hostels.com, info@somniohostels.com).

Apartments in Barceloneta

$ BCNflats rents 40 renovated apartments with kitchens right near
the beach in the lively Barceloneta quarter, the former fishermen's
neighborhood that's become increasingly gentrified (Db-€100 in
June–Aug, €80 Sept–May, up to 2 kids stay free, prices vary with
size—see photos on website, €40 cleaning fee, no minimum-stay
requirement, 10 percent less for 7-night stay, 25 percent deposit
required to reserve online, €150 refundable cash security deposit
collected at check-in, no breakfast, complimentary bottle of *cava*

when you mention this book, Frederick or an associate will meet you to check in—arrange when you reserve, mobile 620-585-594, www.bcnflats.net, info@bcnflats.net). They also have 12 more units in the somewhat seedy Barri Gòtic near the Ramblas (larger, higher prices, same website).

Eating in Barcelona

Barcelona, the capital of Catalan cuisine—featuring seafood—offers a tremendous variety of colorful eateries, ranging from basic and filling to chic and trendy. Because of their common struggles, Catalans seem to have an affinity for Basque culture, so you'll find

a lot of Basque tapas places here, too. Most of my listings are lively spots with a busy tapas scene at the bar, along with restaurant tables for *raciones*. A regional specialty is *pa amb tomaquet* (pah ahm too-MAH-kaht), bread topped with a mix of crushed tomato and olive oil.

I've listed mostly practical, characteristic, colorful, and affordable restaurants. My recommendations are grouped by neighborhood—along the Ramblas; in the Barri Gòtic; in the Ribera neighborhood (best for foodies); and in the Eixample—followed by some budget options scattered throughout the city. Note that many restaurants close in August (or July), when the owners take a vacation.

Restaurants generally serve lunch from 13:00 to 16:00 and dinner from 20:00 until very late (Spaniards don't start dinner until about 21:00). It's deadly to your Barcelona experience to eat too early—if a place feels touristy, come back later and it may be a thriving local favorite.

Along the Ramblas
Within a few steps of the Ramblas you'll find handy lunch places, an inviting market hall, and a slew of vegetarian options.

Lunching Simply yet Memorably near the Ramblas
Although these places are enjoyable for a lunch break during your Ramblas sightseeing, many are also open for dinner.

Taverna Basca Irati serves 40 kinds of hot and cold Basque *pintxos* for €1.80 each. These are open-faced sandwiches—like sushi on bread. Muscle in through the hungry local crowd, get an empty plate from the waiter, and then help yourself. Every few minutes, waiters prance proudly by with a platter of new, still-warm munchies. Grab one as they pass by...it's addictive. You pay on the honor system: You're charged by the number of toothpicks left on your plate when you're done. Wash it down with €2–3 glasses of Rioja (full-bodied red wine), Txakolí (sprightly Basque white wine) or *sidra* (apple wine) poured from on high to add oxygen and bring out the flavor (daily 11:00–24:00, a block off the Ramblas, behind arcade at Carrer Cardenal Casanyes 15, Metro: Liceu, tel. 933-023-084).

Restaurant Elisabets is a happy little neighborhood eatery packed with antique radios, and is popular with locals for its €11 "home-cooked" three-course lunch special. Stop by for lunch, survey what those around you are enjoying, and order what looks best (Mon–Sat 7:30–23:00, closed Sun and Aug, lunch special served 13:00–16:00, otherwise only €3 tapas—not full meals, 2 blocks west of Ramblas on far corner of Plaça Bonsucces at Carrer Elisabets 2, tel. 933-175-826, run by Pilar).

Café Granja Viader is a quaint time capsule, family-run since 1870. They boast about being the first dairy business to bottle and distribute milk in Spain. This feminine-feeling place—specializing in baked and dairy delights, toasted sandwiches, and light meals—is ideal for a traditional breakfast. Or indulge your sweet tooth: Try a glass of *orxata* (or *horchata*—*chufa*-nut milk, summer only), *llet mallorquina* (Majorca-style milk with cinnamon, lemon, and sugar), *crema catalana* (crème brûlée, their specialty), or *suis* ("Swiss"—hot chocolate with a snowcap of whipped cream). *Mel y mato* is fresh cheese with honey...very Catalan (Tue–Sat 9:00–13:45 & 17:00–20:45, Mon 17:00–20:45 only, closed Sun, a block off the Ramblas behind El Carme church at Xucla 4, tel. 933-183-486).

Picnics: Shoestring tourists buy groceries at **El Corte Inglés** (Mon–Sat 10:00–22:00, closed Sun, supermarket in basement, Plaça de Catalunya) and **Carrefour Express supermarket** (Mon–Sat 10:00–22:00, closed Sun, Ramblas 113).

In and near La Boquería Market

Try eating at La Boquería market at least once (#91 on the Ramblas). Like all farmers markets in Europe, this place is ringed by colorful, good-value eateries. Lots of stalls sell fun take-away food—especially fruit salads and fresh-squeezed fruit juices. There are several good bars around the market busy with shoppers munching at the counter (breakfast, tapas all day, coffee). The market, and most of the eateries listed here (unless noted), are open Monday through Saturday from 8:00 until 20:00 (though things get very quiet after about 16:00) and are closed on Sunday.

Pinotxo Bar is just to the right as you enter the market. It's a great spot for coffee, breakfast (spinach tortillas, or whatever's cooking with toast), or tapas. Fun-loving Juan and his family are La Boquería fixtures. Grab a stool across the way to sip your drink with people-watching views. Have a Chucho?

Kiosko Universal is popular for its great prices on wonderful fish dishes. As you enter the market from the Ramblas, it's all the way to the left in the first alley. If you see people waiting, ask who's last in line *("¿El último?")*. You'll eat immersed in the spirit of the market (€14 fixed-price lunches with different fresh-fish options 12:00–16:00, always packed but better before 12:30, tel. 933-178-286).

Restaurant la Gardunya, at the back of the market, offers tasty meat and seafood meals made with fresh ingredients bought directly from the market (€13 fixed-price lunch includes wine and bread, €16 three-course dinner specials don't include wine, €10–20 à la carte dishes, Mon–Sat 13:00–16:00 & 20:00–24:00, closed Sun, mod seating indoors or outside watching the market action, Carrer Jerusalem 18, tel. 933-024-323).

Bar Terrace Restaurant Ra is a lively terrace immediately behind the market (at the right end of the big parking lot) with outdoor tables filled by young, trendy, happy eaters. At lunch they serve one great salad/pasta/wine meal for €11. If you feel like eating a big salad under an umbrella…this is the place (€9–15 à la carte dishes, daily 10:00–12:30 & 13:30–16:00 & 21:00–24:00, fancier menu at night, mobile 615-959-872).

Vegetarian Eateries near Plaça de Catalunya and the Ramblas

Biocenter, a Catalan soup-and-salad restaurant popular with local vegetarians, takes its cooking very seriously and feels a bit more like a real restaurant than most (€6–9.75 weekday lunch specials include soup or salad and plate of the day, €15 dinner specials, Mon–Sat 13:00–23:00, Sun 13:00–16:00, 2 blocks off the Ramblas at Pintor Fortuny 25, Metro: Catalunya, tel. 933-014-583).

Juicy Jones is a tutti-frutti vegan/vegetarian eatery with colorful graffiti decor, a hip veggie menu (served downstairs), groovy laid-back staff, and a stunning array of fresh-squeezed juices served at the bar. Pop in for a quick €3 "juice of the day." For lunch you can get the Indian-inspired €6 *thali* plate, the €6.25 plate of the day, or an €8.50 meal including one of the two plates plus soup or salad and dessert (daily 12:30–23:30, also tapas and salads, Carrer Cardenal Casanyes 7, tel. 933-024-330). There's another location on the other side of the Ramblas (Carrer Hospital 74).

In Barceloneta

La Mar Salada is a traditional seafood restaurant with a slight modern twist, located on the strip leading to the Barceloneta beach. Their à la carte menu includes seafood-and-rice dishes, fresh fish, and homemade deserts. A nice meal will run you about €30–35 per person (€14 fixed-price weekday meal, Wed–Mon 13:00–16:00 & 20:00–23:00, Sat–Sun 13:00–23:00, closed Tue, indoor and outdoor seating, Passeig Joan de Borbó 59, tel. 932-212-127).

In the Barri Gòtic

These eateries populate Barcelona's atmospheric Gothic Quarter, near the cathedral. Choose between a sit-down meal at a restaurant or a string of very old-fashioned tapas bars.

Restaurants in the Barri Gòtic

Café de l'Academia is a delightful place on a pretty square tucked away in the heart of the Barri Gòtic—but patronized mainly by the neighbors. They serve "honest cuisine" from the market with Catalan roots. The candlelit, air-conditioned interior is rustic yet elegant, with soft jazz, flowers, and modern art. And if you want to eat outdoors on a convivial, mellow square...this is the place (€10–12 first courses, €12–15 second courses, fixed-price lunch for €10 at the bar or €14 at a table, Mon–Fri 13:30–16:00 & 20:30–23:30, closed Sat–Sun, near the City Hall square, off Carrer de Jaume I up Carrer Dagueria at Carrer Lledo 1, tel. 933-198-253).

Popular Chain Restaurants: Barcelona enjoys a chain of several bright, modern restaurants. These five are a hit for their modern, artfully presented Spanish and Mediterranean cuisine, crisp ambience, and unbeatable prices. Because of their three-course €9 lunches and €16–20 dinners (both with wine), all are crowded with locals and in-the-know tourists (all open daily 13:00–15:45 & 20:30–23:30, unless otherwise noted). My favorite of the bunch is **La Crema Canela,** which feels cozier than the others and is the only one that takes reservations (opens at 20:00 for dinner, 30 yards north of Plaça Reial at Passatge de Madoz 6, tel. 933-182-744). The rest are notorious for long lines at the door—arrive 30 minutes before opening, or be prepared to wait. Like La Crema Canela, the next two are also within a block of the Plaça Reial: **La Fonda** (opens at 19:00 for dinner, Carrer dels Escudellers 10, very close

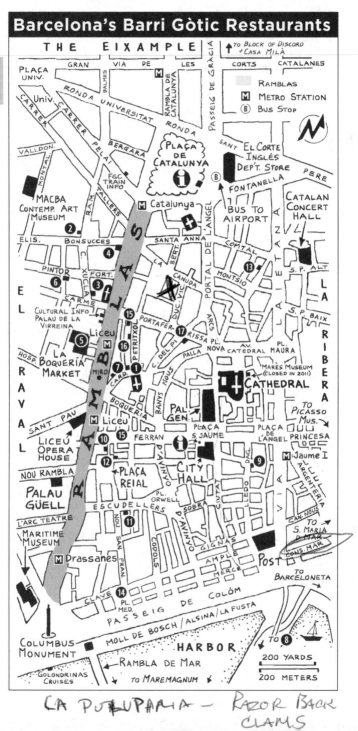

Barcelona's Barri Gòtic Restaurants

CA PUTUPARIA — RAZOR BACK CLAMS

Restaurants Key

1. Taverna Basca Irati
2. Restaurant Elisabets
3. Café Granja Viader
4. Supermarket
5. La Boquería Market Eateries
6. Biocenter Veggie Rest.
7. Juicy Jones
8. To La Mar Salada
9. Café de l'Academia
10. La Crema Canela
11. La Fonda
12. Les Quinze Nits
13. La Dolça Herminia
14. Carrer de la Mercè Tapas Bars
15. Casa Colomina
16. Granja La Pallaresa
17. Fargas Chocolate Shop

to a seedy stretch of street—approach it from the Ramblas rather than from Plaça Reial, tel. 933-017-515) and **Les Quinze Nits** (on Plaça Reial at #6—you'll see the line, tel. 933-173-075). The fourth place, **La Dolça Herminia,** is near the Catalan Concert Hall (2 blocks toward Ramblas from Catalan Concert Hall at Carrer de les Magdalenes 27, tel. 933-170-676). The fifth restaurant in the chain, **La Rita,** is described later, under "Restaurants in the Eixample."

Tapas on Carrer de la Mercè in the Barri Gòtic

Barcelona boasts great *tascas*—colorful local tapas bars. Get small plates (for maximum sampling) by asking for "tapas," not the bigger *"raciones."* Glasses of *vino tinto*  go for about €0.50. And though trendy uptown restaurants are safer, better-lit, and come with English menus and less grease, these places will stain your journal. The neighborhood's dark, the regulars are rough-edged, and you'll get a glimpse of a crusty Barcelona from before the affluence hit. Try *pimientos de padrón*—Russian roulette with peppers that are lightly fried in oil and salted...only a few are jalapeño-spicy. At the cider bars, it's traditional to order *queso de cabrales* (a traditional, very moldy bleu cheese) and spicy chorizo (sausage), ideally prepared *al diablo* ("devil-style")—soaked in wine, then flambéed at your table. Several places serve *leche de pantera* (panther milk)—liquor mixed with milk.

From the bottom of the Ramblas (near the Columbus Monument), hike east along Carrer Clave. Then follow the small street that runs along the right side of the church (Carrer de la Mercè), stopping at the *tascas* that look fun. For a montage of edible memories, wander Carrer de la Mercè west to east and consider these spots, stopping wherever looks most inviting. I've listed ye olde dives, but there are many trendy places here as well. Most of these places close down around 23:00.

La Pulpería (at #16) has a bit less character than the others, but eases you into the scene with fried fish, octopus, and *patatas bravas,* all with Galician Ribeiro wine. Farther down at the corner (#28), **La Plata** keeps things wonderfully simple, serving extremely cheap plates of sardines (€1.70), little salads (€1.50), and small glasses of keg wine (less than €1). **Tasca el Corral** (#17) serves mountain favorites from northern Spain by the half-*ración* (see their list), such as *queso de cabrales* and chorizo *al diablo* with *sidra* (apple wine sold by the €5 bottle). **Sidrería Tasca La Socarrena** (#21) offers hard cider from Asturias in €5 bottles with *queso de cabrales* and chorizo. At the end of Carrer de la Mercè, **Cerveceria Vendimia** slings tasty clams and mussels (hearty *raciones* for €4–6 a plate—they don't do smaller portions, so order sparingly). Sit at the bar and point to what looks good. Their *pulpo* (octopus) is more expensive and is the house specialty. Carrer Ample and Carrer Gignas, the streets parallel to Carrer de la Mercè inland, have more refined bar-hopping possibilities.

In the Ribera District, near the Picasso Museum

La Ribera, the hottest neighborhood in town, sparkles with eclectic and trendy as well as subdued and classy little restaurants hidden in the small lanes surrounding the Church of Santa Maria del Mar. While I've listed a few well-established tapas bars that are great for light meals, to really dine, simply wander around for 15 minutes and pick the place that tickles your gastronomic fancy. I think those who say they know what's best in this area are kidding themselves—it's changing too fast and the choices are too personal. One thing's for sure: There are a lot of talented and hardworking restaurateurs with plenty to offer. Consider starting your evening off with a glass of fine wine at one of the *enotecas* on the square facing the Church of Santa Maria del Mar. Sit back and admire the pure Catalan Gothic architecture. My first three listings are all on the main drag, Carrer de l'Argenteria.

Sagardi offers a wonderful array of Basque goodies—tempting *pinchos* and *montaditos* at €1.80 each—along its huge bar. Ask for a plate and graze (just take whatever looks good). You can sit on the square with your plunder for 20 percent extra. Wash it down with Txakolí, a Basque white wine poured from the spout of a huge wooden barrel into a glass as you watch. When you're done, they'll count your toothpicks to tally your bill (daily 12:00–24:00, Carrer de l'Argenteria 62–64, tel. 933-199-993).

Sagardi Euskal Taberna, hiding behind the thriving Sagardi tapas bar (described above), is a mod, rustic, and minimalist woody restaurant committed to serving Basque T-bone steaks and grilled specialties with only the best ingredients. Crisp, friendly service and a big open kitchen with sizzling grills contribute to the ambience. Reservations are smart (€10–20 first courses, €20–30 second courses, plan on €45 for dinner, daily 13:00–16:00 & 20:00–24:00, Carrer de l'Argenteria 62, tel. 933-199-993).

Taller de Tapas ("Tapas Workshop") is an upscale, trendier tapas bar and restaurant that dishes up well-presented, sophisticated morsels and light meals in a medieval-stone yet mod setting. Pay 10 percent more to sit on the square. Elegant, but a bit stuffy, it's favored by local office workers who aren't into the Old World Gothic stuff. Four plates will fill a hungry diner for about €20 (daily 8:30–24:00, Carrer de l'Argenteria 51, tel. 932-688-559).

El Xampanyet, a colorful family-run bar with a fun-loving staff (Juan Carlos, his mom, and the man who may be his father), specializes in tapas and anchovies. Don't be put off by the seafood from a tin: Catalans like it this way. A *sortido* (assorted plate) of *carne* (meat) or *pescado* (fish) with *pa amb tomaquet* (bread with crushed-tomato spread) makes for a fun meal. It's filled with tourists during the sightseeing day, but this is a local favorite after dark. The scene is great but—especially during busy times—it's tough without Spanish skills. When I asked about the price, Juan Carlos said, "Who cares? The ATM is just across the street." Plan on spending €20 for a meal with wine (same price at bar or table, Tue–Sat 12:00–16:00 & 19:00–23:30, Sun 12:00–16:00 only, closed Mon, a half-block beyond the Picasso Museum at Montcada 22, tel. 933-197-003).

In the Eixample

The people-packed boulevards of the Eixample (Passeig de Gràcia and Rambla de Catalunya) are lined with appetizing eateries featuring breezy outdoor seating. Choose between a real restaurant or an upscale tapas bar.

Restaurants in the Eixample

La Rita is a fresh and dressy little restaurant serving Catalan cuisine near the Block of Discord. Their lunches (three courses with wine for €8, Mon–Fri 13:00–15:45) and dinners (€15, à la carte, daily 20:30–23:30) are a great value. Like most of its sister restaurants—described under "Dining in the Barri Gòtic," earlier—it takes no reservations and its prices attract long lines, so arrive just before the doors open...or wait (a block from Metro: Passeig de Gràcia, near corner of Carrer de Pau Claris and Carrer Arago at Arago 279, tel. 934-872-376).

La Bodegueta is an atmospheric below-street-level bodega serving hearty wines, homemade vermouth, *anchoas* (anchovies), tapas, and *flautas*—sandwiches made with flute-thin baguettes. Its daily €12 lunch special of three courses with wine is served 13:00–16:00. A long block from Gaudí's Casa Milà, this makes a fine sightseeing break (Mon–Sat 8:00–24:00, Sun 19:00–24:00, at intersection with Provenza, Rambla de Catalunya 100, Metro: Provença, tel. 932-154-894).

Restaurante la Palmera serves a mix of Catalan, Mediterranean, and French cuisine in an elegant yet smoky room with bottle-lined walls. The smoke keeps out the tourists. This place offers great food, service, and value—for me, a very special meal in Barcelona. They have three zones: the classic main room, a more forgettable adjacent room, and a few outdoor tables. I like the classic room. Reservations are smart (€12 plates, creative €16 six-plate *degustation* lunch, Tue–Sat 13:00–15:45 & 20:30–23:15, closed Sun–Mon, Enric Granados 57, at the corner with Mallorca, tel. 934-532-338).

Restaurant Flauta fills two floors with enthusiastic eaters (I prefer the ground floor). It's fresh and modern, with a fun, no-stress menu featuring €5 small plates, creative €4 *flauta* sandwiches, and a €12.50 three-course lunch deal including a drink. Good €2.30 wines by the glass are listed on the blackboard. This is a place to order high on the menu for a satisfying, moderately priced meal (Mon–Sat 13:00–24:00, closed Sun, fun-loving and helpful staff recommends the fried vegetables, no reservations, just off Via Diputació at d'Aribau 23, tel. 933-237-038).

Cinc Sentits ("Five Senses"), with only about 30 seats, is my gourmet recommendation. It's a chic, minimalist, smoke-free, but slightly snooty place where all the attention goes to the fine service and elegantly presented dishes. It's run by Catalans who lived in Canada (so there's absolutely no language barrier) and serve avant-garde cuisine inspired by Catalan traditions and ingredients. Their €49 and €69 *degustation menus* are unforgettable extravaganzas. Reservations are required (Tue–Sat 13:30–15:00 & 20:30–23:00, closed Sun–Mon, near Carrer d'Aragó at d'Aribau 58, tel. 933-239-490).

El Racó is a local favorite for "creative Mediterranean cuisine"—pasta, pizza, crêpes, and salads (about €7–9 each) in a modern, lively, cavernous-but-bright, air-conditioned setting (daily 13:00–24:00, Rambla de Catalunya 25, tel. 933-175-688).

A Bit Farther Out: **Hofmann** is a renowned cooking school with an excellent if pricey restaurant serving modern Mediterranean market cuisine. Dress up and dine in intimate rooms papered with photos of famous patrons. The four-course €40 lunches are made up of just what the students are working on that day—so there's no choice (watch the students as they cook). Dinners can easily cost twice as much (à la carte). Save room (and euros) for the incredible desserts. Reserve long in advance, because locals love this place (Mon–Fri 13:30–15:15 & 21:00–23:15, closed Sat–Sun and Aug, 4 blocks northwest of Casa Milà at La Granada del Penedès 14–16, tel. 932-187-165, www.hofmann-bcn.com).

Tapas Bars in the Eixample

Many trendy and touristic tapas bars in the Eixample offer a cheery welcome and slam out the appetizers. These three are my favorites.

Quasi Queviures (**"Qu Qu"** for short) serves upscale tapas, sandwiches, or the whole nine yards—classic food served fast from a fun menu with modern decor and a high-energy sports-bar ambience. It's bright, clean, and not too crowded. Walk through their enticing kitchen to get to the tables in back. Committed to developing a loyal following, they claim, "We fertilize our local customers with daily specialties" (€2–5 tapas, €5 dinner salads, €8 plates, prices 17 percent higher on the terrace, daily 8:00–24:00, between Gran Via and Via Diputació at Passeig de Gràcia 24, tel. 933-174-512).

Ciudad Condal Cerveceria brags that it serves the best *montaditos* (€2–3 little open-faced sandwiches) and beers in Barcelona. It's an Eixample favorite, with an elegant bar and tables plus good seating out on the Rambla de Catalunya for all that people-watching action. It's classier than Qu Qu and packed after 21:00, when you'll likely need to put your name on a list and wait. While it has no restaurant-type menu, the list of tapas and *montaditos* is easy, fun, and comes with a great variety (including daily specials). This place is a cut above your normal tapas bar, but with reasonable prices (most tapas around €4–5, daily until 24:00, facing the intersection of Gran Via and Rambla de Catalunya at Rambla de Catalunya 18, tel. 933-181-997).

La Tramoia, at the opposite corner from Ciudad Condal Cerveceria, serves piles of cheap *montaditos* and tapas at its ground-floor bar and at nice tables inside and out. If Ciudad Condal Cerveceria is jammed, you're more likely to find a seat here. The brasserie-style restaurant upstairs bustles with happy local eaters enjoying grilled meats (€6–15 plates), but I'd stay downstairs for the €4–8 tapas (open daily, also facing the intersection of Gran Via and Rambla de Catalunya at Rambla de Catalunya 15, tel. 934-123-634).

Budget Options Around Town

Bright, clean, and inexpensive sandwich shops proudly hold the cultural line against the fast-food invasion hamburgerizing the rest of Europe. Catalan sandwiches are made to order with crunchy French bread. Rather than butter, locals prefer *toma-quet* (a spread of crushed tomatoes). You'll see two big local chains (Pans & Company and Bocatta) every-where, but these serve mass-produced McBaguettes ordered from a multilin-

gual menu. I've had better luck with hole-in-the-wall sandwich shops—virtually as numerous as the chains—where you can see exactly what you're getting. Kebab places are another good, super-cheap standby.

A Short, Sweet Walk

Let me propose this three-stop dessert (or, since these places close well before the traditional Barcelona dinnertime, a late-afternoon snack). You'll try a refreshing glass of *orxata*, munch some *churros con chocolate*, and visit a fine *xocolateria*, all within a three-minute walk of one another in the Barri Gòtic just off the Ramblas. Start at the corner of Carrer Portaferrissa midway down the Ramblas. For the best atmosphere, begin your walk at about 18:00 (note that the last place is closed on Sun).

Turrón at **Casa Colomina:** Walk down Carrer Portaferrissa to #8 (on the right). Casa Colomina, founded in 1908, specializes in homemade *turróns*—a variation of nougat made with almond, honey, and sugar, brought to Spain by the Moors 1,200 years ago. Three different kinds are sold in big €12 slabs: *blando, duro,* and *yema*—soft, hard, and yolk (€2 smaller chunks also available). In the summer, the shop also sells ice cream and the refreshing *orxata* (or *horchata*—a drink made from the *chufa* nut). Order a glass and ask to see and eat a *chufa* nut (a.k.a. earth almond or tiger nut; Mon–Sat 10:00–20:30, Sun 12:30–20:30, tel. 933-122-511).

Churros con Chocolate at **Granja La Pallaresa:** Continue down Carrer Portaferrissa, taking a right at Carrer Petritxol to this fun-loving *xocolateria*. Older, elegant ladies gather here for the Spanish equivalent of tea time—dipping their greasy *churros* into pudding-thick cups of hot chocolate (€4.10 for five *churros con chocolate*, Mon–Fri 9:00–13:00 & 16:00–21:00, Sat–Sun 9:00–13:00

& 17:00–21:00, Carrer Petritxol 11, tel. 933-022-036).

Homemade Chocolate at Fargas: For your last stop, head for the ornate Fargas chocolate shop. Continue down Carrer Petritxol to the square, hook left through the two-part square, and then left up Carrer del Pi—it's on the corner of Portaferrissa and Carrer del Pi. Since the 19th century, gentlemen with walking canes have dropped by here for their chocolate fix. Founded in 1827, this is one of the oldest and most traditional chocolate shops in Barcelona. If they're not too busy, ask to see the old chocolate mill *("¿Puedo ver el molino?")* to the right of the counter. They sell even tiny quantities (one little morsel) by the weight, so don't be shy. A delicious chunk of the crumbly semi-sweet house specialty costs €0.45 (tray by the mill). The tempting bonbons in the window cost about €1 each (Mon–Fri 9:30–13:30 & 16:00–20:00, Sat 10:00–14:00 & 16:00–20:00, closed Sun, tel. 933-020-342).

Barcelona Connections

By Train

Unless otherwise noted, all of these trains depart from the Sants Station; however, some trains also stop at other stations more convenient to the downtown tourist zone: França Station, Passeig de Gràcia, or Plaça de Catalunya. Figure out if your train stops at these stations (and board there) to save yourself the trip to Sants.

The **AVE train to Madrid** has shaved hours off that journey, making it faster than flying (when you consider that you're zipping from downtown to downtown). The train departs almost hourly. The nonstop train is a little more expensive (€135, 2.5–3 hours) than the slightly slower train that makes a few stops and adds about a half-hour (€115, 3.5 hours). Regular reserved AVE tickets can be prepurchased at www.renfe.com and picked up at the station. If you have a railpass, you'll pay only a reservation fee of €25 for first class, which includes a meal (€15 second class, buy at any train station in Spain). Passholders can't reserve online through RENFE but can make the reservation at www.raileurope.com for delivery before leaving the US ($17 in second class, $40 in first class).

From Barcelona by Train to: Sitges (4/hour, 30–35 minutes, €3), **Montserrat** (departs from Plaça d'Espanya, hourly, 1.5 hours, €16 round-trip, includes cable car or rack train to monastery), **Figueres** (hourly, 2 hours, €30 round-trip), **Sevilla** (3/day—two fast, 5.5 hours, €140; one slow, 12 hours, €62), **Granada** (1/day Wed, Fri, and Sun only, 11.5 hours, €61; also 1 night train/day, 12 hours, €63), **Salamanca** (8/day, 6–7.5 hours, change in Madrid from Atocha Station to Chamartín Station via Metro; 1 direct/day, 11.25 hours), **San Sebastián** (2/day, 5.5 hours, €62), **Málaga**

(3/day—two fast, 5.5 hours, €140; one slow, 13 hours, €63), **Lisbon** (no direct trains, head to Madrid and then catch night train to Lisbon, 17 hours, about €100), **Nice** (1/day via Montpelier, about €100; cheaper connections possible with multiple changes including Cerbère), **Avignon** (5/day, fewer on weekends, 6–9 hours, about €40, or about €65 for change in Montpellier), **Paris** (3/day, 9 hours, 1–2 changes; 1 night train/day, 12 hours, about €200, or €50 with railpass, reservation mandatory). Train info: toll tel. 902-320-320, www.renfe.com.

By Bus

Destinations include **Madrid** (14/day, 8 hours, €28—a fraction of the AVE train price, departs from Nord bus station at Metro: Arc de Triomf on line 1, bus info toll tel. 902-260-606, Alsa bus company toll tel. 902-422-242), **Salamanca** (4/day, 11 hours, Alsa buses), and **Cadaqués** (2/day, 2.75 hours, €21). Sarfa buses serve all the **coastal resorts** (tel. toll 902-302-025, www.sarfa.com). For bus schedules, see www.barcelonanord.com.

By Plane

Check the reasonable flights from Barcelona to Sevilla or Madrid. Vueling is Iberia's most popular discount airline (e.g., Barcelona–Madrid flights as low as €40 if booked in advance, toll tel. 902-333-933, www.vueling.com). Iberia (toll tel. 902-400-500, www.iberia.com) and Air Europa (toll tel. 902-401-501 or 932-983-907, www.aireuropa.com) offer €80 flights to Madrid. Also, for flights to other parts of Europe, consider British Airways (toll tel. 902-111-333, www.britishairways.com), easyJet (toll tel. 902-299-992, www.easyjet.com), and Ryanair (www.ryanair.com).

Most flights use Barcelona's **El Prat de Llobregat Airport** (tel. 913-211-000). Its two terminals serve both domestic and international flights and are linked by shuttle buses. Air France, Air Europa, American, British, Continental, Iberia, Lufthansa, Spanair, US Airways, Vueling, and others use the newer terminal 1. EasyJet, Delta, and minor airlines use terminal 2. Ryanair uses a smaller airstrip 60 miles away, called **Girona-Costa Brava Airport** (tel. 972-186-600). Information on both airports can be found on the official Spanish airport website, www.aena.es.

NEAR BARCELONA

Figueres • Cadaqués • Sitges • Montserrat

Four fine sights are day-trip temptations from Barcelona. Fans of Surrealism can combine a fantasy in Dalí-land by stopping at the Dalí Theater-Museum in Figueres (about two hours from Barcelona) and spending a day or two in the classy but sleepy port-town getaway of Cadaqués (pictured above, an hour from Figueres; note that the Salvador Dalí House in Cadaqués requires reservations to visit). For the consummate day at the beach, head 45 minutes south to the charming and free-spirited resort town of Sitges. Pilgrims with hiking boots head an hour into the mountains for the most sacred spot in Catalunya: Montserrat.

Figueres

The town of Figueres (feeg-YEHR-ehs)—conveniently connected by train to Barcelona—is of sightseeing interest only for its Salvador Dalí Theater-Museum. In fact, the entire town seems Dalí-dominated.

Getting to Figueres: Figueres is an easy day trip from Barcelona, or a handy stopover en route to France (trains between Barcelona and France stop in Figueres). Trains to Figueres from Barcelona depart from Sants Station or from the RENFE Station at Metro: Passeig de Gràcia (hourly, 2 hours, €30 round-trip).

Arrival in Figueres: From the train station, simply follow *Museu Dalí* signs (and the crowds) for the 15-minute walk to the museum.

Near Barcelona

FRANCE

SPAIN

TO COLLIOURE & PERPIGNAN

CERBÈRE
PORTBOU
PORT LLIGAT
FIGUERES
CADAQUÉS
ROSES
GIRONA-COSTA BRAVA
GIRONA
PÚBOL
MACANET
COSTA BRAVA
TOSSA
BLANES
MANRESA
CREMALLERA RACK RAILWAY
MONISTROL DE MONT.
MONT.-AERI
MONT-SERRAT
CABLE CAR
VILA-FRANCA
TO MADRID
SITGES
BARCELONA
EL PRAT DE LLOBREGAT AIRPORT
COSTA DAURADA
DCH

+++ RAIL
--- BUS

50 MILES
50 KM

Sights in Figueres

▲▲▲Dalí Theater-Museum (Teatre-Museu Dalí)

This is *the* essential Dalí sight—and, if you like Dalí, one of Europe's most enjoyable museums, period. Inaugurated in 1974, the museum is a work of art in itself. Ever the entertainer and promoter, Dalí personally conceptualized, designed, decorated, and painted it to showcase his life's work. The museum fills a former theater and is the artist's mausoleum (his tomb is in the crypt below center stage). It's also a kind of mausoleum to Dalí's creative spirit.

Dalí had his first public art showing at age 14 here in this building when it was a theater, and he was baptized in the church just across the street. The place was sentimental to him. After the theater was destroyed in the Spanish Civil War, Dalí struck a deal with the mayor: Dalí would rebuild the theater as a museum to his works, Figueres would be put on the sightseeing map...and the money's been flowing in ever since.

Even the building's exterior—painted pink, studded with golden loaves of bread, and topped with monumental eggs and a geodesic dome—exudes Dalí's outrageous public persona.

Cost and Hours: €11; July–Sept daily 9:00–20:00; Oct and March–June Tue–Sun 9:30–18:00, closed Mon; Nov–Feb Tue–Sun 10:30–18:00, closed Mon; last entry 45 minutes before closing, tel. 972-677-500, www.salvador-dali.org. No flash photography. The free bag check has your belongings waiting for you at the exit.

Coin-Op Tip: Much of Dalí's art is movable and coin-operated—bring a few €0.20 and €0.50 coins.

Visiting the Museum: The museum has two parts: the theater-mausoleum and the "Dalí's Jewels" exhibit in an adjacent building. There's no logical order for a visit (that would be un-Surrealistic), and the museum can be mobbed at times. Naturally, there's no audioguide. Dalí said there are two kinds of visitors: those who don't need a description, and those who aren't worth a description.

◐ Self-Guided Tour: At the risk of offending Dalí, I've written this loose commentary to attach some meaning to your visit.

Stepping into the **theater** (with its audience of statues), face the stage—and Dalí's unmarked crypt. You know how you can never get a cab when it's raining? Pop a coin into Dalí's personal 1941 Cadillac, and it rains inside the car. Look above, atop the tire tower: That's the boat Dalí enjoyed with his soul mate, Gala—his emotional life preserver, who kept him from going overboard. When she died, so did he (for his last seven years). Blue tears made of condoms drip below the boat.

Up on the **stage,** squint at the big digital Abraham Lincoln, and president #16 comes into focus. Approach the painting to find that Abe's facial cheeks are Gala's butt cheeks. Under the painting, a door leads to the **Treasures Room,** with the greatest collection of actual Dalí original oil paintings in the museum. (Many of those you see on the walls are prints.) You'll see Cubist visions of Cadaqués and dreamy portraits of Gala. Crutches—a recurring Dalí theme—represent Gala, who kept him supported whenever a meltdown threatened.

The famous **Homage to Mae West room** is a tribute to the sultry seductress. Dalí loved her attitude. Saying things like, "Why marry and make one man unhappy, when you can stay single and make so many so happy?" Mae West was to conventional morality what Dalí

Salvador Dalí
(1904–1989)

When Salvador Dalí was asked, "Are you on drugs?" he replied, "I am the drug...take me."

Labeled by various critics as sick, greedy, paranoid, arrogant, and a clown, Dalí produced some of the most thought-provoking and trailblazing art of the 20th century. His erotic, violent, disjointed imagery continues to disturb and intrigue today.

Born in Figueres to a well-off family, Dalí showed talent early. He was expelled from Madrid's prestigious art school—twice—but formed longtime friendships with playwright Federico García Lorca and filmmaker Luis Buñuel.

After a breakthrough art exhibit in Barcelona in 1925, Dalí moved to Paris. He hobnobbed with fellow Spaniards Pablo Picasso and Joan Miró, along with a group of artists exploring Sigmund Freud's theory that we all have a hidden part of our mind, the unconscious "id," that surfaces when we dream. Dalí became the best-known spokesman for this group of Surrealists, channeling his id to create photorealistic dream images (melting watches, burning giraffes) set in bizarre dreamscapes.

His life changed forever in 1929, when he met an older, married Russian woman named Gala who would become his wife, muse, model, manager, and emotional compass. Dalí's popularity spread to the US, where he (and Gala) weathered the WWII years.

was to conventional art. Climb to the vantage point where the sofa lips, fireplace nostrils, painting eyes, and drapery hair come together to make the face of Mae West.

Dalí's art can be playful, but also disturbing. He was passionate about the dark side of things, but with Gala for balance, he managed never to go off the deep end. Unlike Pablo Casals (the Catalan cellist) and Pablo Picasso (another local artist), Dalí didn't go into exile under Franco's dictatorship. Pragmatically, he accepted both Franco and the Church, and was supported by the dictator. Apart from the occasional *sardana* dance, you won't find a hint of politics in Dalí's art.

Wander around. You can spend hours here, wondering, is it real or not real? Am I crazy, or is it you? Beethoven is painted with squid ink applied by a shoe on a stormy night. Jesus is made with candle smoke and an eraser. It's fun to see the Dalí-ization of art

In his prime, Dalí's work became less Surrealist and more classical, influenced by past masters of painted realism (Velázquez, Raphael, Ingres) and by his own study of history, science, and religion. He produced large-scale paintings of historical events (e.g., Columbus discovering America, the Last Supper) that were collages of realistic scenes floating in a surrealistic landscape, peppered with thought-provoking symbols.

Dalí—an extremely capable technician—mastered many media, including film. *An Andalusian Dog* (*Un Chien Andalou*, 1929, with Luis Buñuel) was a cutting-edge montage of disturbing, eyeball-slicing images. He designed Alfred Hitchcock's big-eye backdrop for the dream sequence of *Spellbound* (1945). He made jewels for the rich and clothes for Coco Chanel, wrote a novel and an autobiography, and pioneered what would come to be called "installations." He also helped develop "performance art" by showing up at an opening in a diver's suit or by playing the role he projected to the media—a super-confident, waxed-mustached artistic genius.

In later years Dalí's over-the-top public image contrasted with his ever-growing illness, depression, and isolation. He endured the scandal of a dealer overselling "limited editions" of his work. When Gala died in 1982, Dalí retreated to his hometown, living his last days in the Torre Galatea of the Theater-Museum complex, where he died of heart failure.

Dalí's legacy as an artist includes his self-marketing persona, his exceptional ability to draw, his provocative pairing of symbols, and his sheer creative drive.

classics. Dalí, like so many modern artists, was inspired by the masters—especially Velázquez.

The former theater's **smoking lounge** is a highlight, displaying portraits of Gala and Dalí (with a big eye, big ear, and a dark side) bookending a Roman candle of creativity. The fascinating ceiling painting shows the feet of Gala and Dalí as they bridge earth and the heavens. Dalí's drawers are wide open and empty, indicating that he gave everything to his art.

Leaving the theater, keep your ticket and pop into the adjacent **"Dalí's Jewels"** exhibit. It shows sketches and paintings of jewelry Dalí designed, and the actual pieces jewelers made from those surreal visions: a mouth full of pearly whites, a golden finger corset, a fountain of diamonds, and the breathing heart. Explore the ambiguous perception worked into the big painting titled *Apotheosis of the Dollar.*

Cadaqués

Since the late 1800s, Cadaqués (kah-dah-KEHS) has served as a haven for intellectuals and artists alike. The fishing village's craggy coastline, sun-drenched colors, and laid-back lifestyle inspired Fauvists such as Henri Matisse and Surrealists such as René Magritte, Marcel Duchamp, and Federico García Lorca. Even Picasso, drawn to this enchanting coastal haunt, painted some of his Cubist works here.

Salvador Dalí, raised in nearby Figueres, brought international fame to this sleepy Catalan port in the 1920s. As a kid Dalí spent summers here in the family cabin, where he was inspired by the rocky landscape that would later be the backdrop for many Surrealist canvases. In 1929 he met his future wife, Gala, in Cadaqués. Together they converted a fisherman's home in nearby Port Lligat into their semi-permanent residence, dividing their time between New York, Paris, and Cadaqués. And it was here that Dalí did his best work.

In spite of its fame, Cadaqués is mellow and feels off the beaten path. If you want a peaceful beach-town escape near Barcelona, this is a good place. From the moment you descend into the town, taking in whitewashed buildings and deep blue waters, you'll be struck by the port's tranquility and beauty. Join the locals playing chess or cards at the cavernous Casino Coffee House (harborfront, with games and Internet access). Have a glass of *vino tinto* or *cremat* (a traditional rum-and-coffee drink served flambé-style) at one of the seaside cafés. Savor the lapping waves, brilliant sun, and gentle breeze. And, for sightseeing, the reason to come to Cadaqués is the Salvador Dalí House, a 20-minute walk from the town center at Port Lligat.

Tourist Information: The TI is at Carrer Cotxe 2 (July–Sept Mon–Sat 9:00–21:00, Sun 10:00–13:00, shorter hours off-season plus closed for lunch, tel. 972-258-315).

Getting to Cadaqués

Reaching Cadaqués is very tough without a car. There are no trains and only a few buses a day.

By Car: It's a twisty drive from Figueres (figure 45–60 minutes). In Cadaqués, drivers should park in the big lot just above the city—don't try to park near the harborfront. To reach the Salvador Dalí House, follow signs near Cadaqués to Port Lligat (easy parking).

By Bus: Cadaqués is connected by Sarfa buses to **Figueres** (3/day, 1 hour, €5.80) and to **Barcelona** (2/day, more in July–Aug, 2.75 hours, €21.35). Bus info: Barcelona toll tel. 902-302-025, Cadaqués tel. 972-258-713, Figueres tel. 972-674-298, www.sarfa.com.

Sights near Cadaqués

In Port Lligat

▲▲▲**Salvador Dalí House (Casa Museu Salvador Dalí)**—
Once Dalí's home, this house gives fans a chance to explore his

labyrinthine compound. This is the best artist's house I've toured in Europe. It shows how a home can really reflect the creative spirit of an artistic genius and his muse. The ambience, both inside and out, is perfect for a Surrealist hanging out with his creative playmate. The bay is ringed by sleepy islands. Fishing boats are jumbled on the beach. After the fishermen painted their boats, Dalí asked them to clean their brushes on his door—creating an abstract work of art he adored (which you'll see as you line up to get your ticket).

The interior is left almost precisely as it was in 1982, when Gala died and Dalí moved out. See Dalí's studio (the clever easel cranks up and down to allow the artist to paint while seated, as he did eight hours a day); the bohemian-yet-divine living room (complete with a mirror to reflect the sunrise onto their bed each morning); the phallic-shaped swimming pool, which was the scene of orgiastic parties; and the painter's study (with his favorite mustaches all lined up). Like Dalí's art, his home is offbeat, provocative, and fun.

Cost and Hours: €10; mid-June–mid-Sept daily 9:30–21:00; mid-Feb–mid-June and mid-Sept–early Jan Tue–Sun 10:30–18:00, closed Mon; closed early Jan–mid-Feb. Last tour departs 50 minutes before closing.

Touring the House: Reservations are mandatory—call or go online in advance to book a time (tel. 972-251-015, www.salvador -dali.org). Only 8–10 people are allowed in (no large groups) every 10 minutes. In summer, book a week in advance. You must arrive 30 minutes early to pick up your ticket, or they'll sell it. Once inside, there are five sections, each with a guard who gives you a brief explanation in English, and then turns you loose for a few minutes. The entire visit takes 50 minutes. Before your tour, enjoy the 15-minute video that plays in the waiting lounge (with walls covered in Dalí media coverage) just across the lane from the house.

Getting There: Parking is free nearby. There are no buses or taxis. The house is a 20-minute, one-mile walk over the hill from Cadaqués to Port Lligat. (The path, which cuts across the isthmus, is much shorter than the road.)

Sleep Code

(€1 = about $1.25, country code: 34)
S = Single, **D** = Double/Twin, **T** = Triple, **Q** = Quad, **b** = bathroom, **s** = shower only. Unless otherwise noted, credit cards are accepted and English is spoken.

To help you easily sort through these listings, I've divided the rooms into two categories, based on the price for a standard double room with bath (during high season):

$$ Higher Priced—Most rooms €85 or more.
$ Lower Priced—Most rooms less than €85.

Prices can change without notice; verify the hotel's current rates online or by email. For other updates, see www .ricksteves.com/update.

Sleeping in Cadaqués

$$ Hotel Llané Petit, with 37 spacious rooms (half with view balconies), is a small resort-like hotel with its own little beach, a 10-minute walk south of the town center (Db-€124 mid-July–Aug, €92 in shoulder season, €59 in winter, €35 more for sea-view rooms, air-con, elevator, Dr. Bartomeus 37, tel. 972-251-020, fax 972-258-778, www.llanepetit.com, info@llanepetit.com). Reserve direct with this book to get a free €12 breakfast (not valid on weekends and mid-July–Aug).

$ Hotel Nou Estrelles is a big concrete exercise in efficient, economic comfort. Facing the bus stop a few blocks in from the waterfront, this family-run hotel offers 15 rooms at a great value (Db-€85 in high season, €60–74 in shoulder season, €55 in winter, extra bed-€10, breakfast-€7, air-con, elevator, Carrer Sant Vicens, tel. 972-259-100, http://hotelnouestrelles.com, nouestrelles @yahoo.es, Emma).

$ Hostal Marina is a cheap, low-energy place, with 27 rooms and a great location a block from the harborfront main square (high season: D-€55, Db-€80; low season: D-€40, Db-€50; balcony rooms-€10 extra, no breakfast, no elevator, no English, Riera 3, tel. 972-159-091).

Eating in Cadaqués

There are plenty of eateries along the beach. A lane called Carrer Miguel Rosset (across from Hotel La Residencia) also has several places worth considering. At **Casa Anita** you'll sit with others around a big table and enjoy house specialties such as *calamares a* *la plancha* (grilled squid) and homemade *helado* (ice cream). Finish your meal with a glass of sweet Muscatel (closed Mon, Calle Miquel Rosset 16, tel. 972-258-471, Juan and family).

Sitges

Sitges (SEE-juhz) is one of Catalunya's most popular resort towns. Because the town beautifully mingles sea and light, it's long

been an artists' colony. Here you can still feel the soul of the Modernistas...in the architecture, the museums, the salty sea breeze, and the relaxed rhythm of life.

Today's Sitges is a world-renowned vacation destination among the gay community. Despite its jet-set status, the Old Town has managed to retain its charm. With a much slower pulse than Barcelona, Sitges is an enjoyable break from the big city.

If you visit during one of Sitges' two big **festivals** (St. Bartholomew on Aug 24 and St. Tecla on Sept 23), you may see teams of *castellars* competing to build human pyramids.

Getting to Sitges: Southbound trains depart Barcelona from Sants Station (take *cercanías* train on the dark green line number 2 toward Sant Vincenç de Calders, 4/hour, 30–35 minutes, €3 each way). Closer to Barcelona's city center, you can catch this same train at the Passeig de Gràcia RENFE Station.

Orientation to Sitges

Tourist Information

The **main TI** is a couple of blocks northwest of the train station (mid-June–mid-Sept Mon–Sat 9:00–20:00, closed Sun; mid-Sept–mid-June Mon–Fri 9:00–14:00 & 16:00–18:30, closed Sat–Sun; Sínia Morera 1). Convenient branch kiosks are in front of the **train station** (mid-June–mid-Sept daily 9:00–13:00 & 17:00–21:00, closed off-season) and down at the start of the **beach promenade** (mid-June–mid-Sept Mon–Sat 10:00–14:00 & 16:00–20:00, Sun 10:00–14:00; mid-Sept–mid-June daily 10:00–14:00 plus Fri–Sat 16:00–19:00). Sitges' TIs share the same phone number (toll tel. 902-103-428) and website (www.sitgestur.com). At any TI, pick up the good map (with info on sights on the back) and brochures for any museums that interest you. The TI can also help you find a room.

Arrival in Sitges

From the train station, exit straight ahead (past a TI kiosk—open in summer) and walk down Carrer Francesc Gumà. When it dead-ends, continue right onto Carrer de Jesús, which takes you to the town's tiny main square, Plaça del Cap de la Villa. (Keep an eye out for directional signs.) From here turn right down Carrer Major ("Main Street"), which leads you past the old market hall (now an art gallery) and the town hall, to a beautiful terrace next to the main church. Poke into the Old Town or take the grand staircase down to the beach promenade.

Sights in Sitges

Sitges basically has two attractions: Its tight-and-tiny Old Town (with a few good museums) and its long, luxurious beaches.

Old Town—Take time to explore the Old Town's narrow streets. They're crammed with cafés, boutiques, and all the resort staples.

The focal point, on the waterfront, is the 17th-century Baroque-style **Sant Bartomeu i Santa Tecla Church.** The terrace in front of the church will help you get the lay of the land.

As an art town, Sitges has seen its share of creative people—some of whom have left their mark in the form of appealing museums. Walking along the water behind the church, you'll find two of the town's three museums, which unfortunately will likely be closed for the next couple of years. When open, the **Museu Maricel** displays the eclectic artwork of a local collector, including some Modernista works, pieces by local Sitges artists, and a collection of maritime-themed works. The **Museu Cau Ferrat** bills itself as a "temple of art," as collected by local intellectual Santiago Rusiñol. In addition to paintings and drawings, there's ironwork, glass, and ceramics. Also on this square, you'll see **Palau Maricel**—a sumptuous old mansion that's sometimes open to the public for concerts in the summer (ask at TI).

The third museum, which will remain open during the closure of the first two, is the **Museu Romàntic.** Offering a look at 19th-century bourgeois lifestyles in an elegant mansion, the museum is a few blocks up (one block west of main square: Head out of the square on the main pedestrian street, then take the first right turn, to Sant Gaudenci 1). Inside, amidst gilded hallways, you'll find a collection of more than 400 dolls (€3.50; July–Sept Tue–Sat 9:30–14:00 & 16:00–19:00, Sun 10:00–15:00, closed Mon;

Oct–June Tue–Sat 9:30–14:00 & 15:30–18:30, Sun 10:00–15:00, closed Mon).

Beaches—Nine beaches, separated by breakwaters, extend about a mile southward from town. Stroll down the seaside promenade, which stretches from the town to the end of the beaches. Anyone can enjoy the sun, sea, and sand; or you can rent a beach chair to relax like a pro. The crowds thin out about halfway down, and the last three beaches are more intimate and cove-like. Along the way, restaurants and *chiringuitos* (beachfront bars) serve tapas, paella, and drinks.

If you walk all the way to the end, you can continue inland to enjoy the nicely landscaped **Terramar Gardens** (Jardins de Terramar; free, daily mid-June–mid-Sept 10:30–20:30, mid-Sept–mid-June 9:00–19:00).

Sleeping in Sitges

Because it's an in-demand resort town, hotel values are not much better here than in Barcelona (especially in summer). But if you prefer a swanky beach town to a big city, consider these options. Note that this is a party town, so expect some noise after hours (request a quiet room). I've listed peak-season prices (roughly mid-July–mid-Sept); these drop substantially off-season. The first one is on the beach, whereas the other two are old villas with colorful tile floors a few blocks into town.

$$ Hotel Celimar, with 26 small but modern rooms, occupies a classic Modernista building facing the beach (Db-€150, €20 extra for sea view, average price off-season-€100, check website for latest prices, air-con, elevator, free Wi-Fi, Paseo de la Ribera 20, tel. 938-110-170, fax 938-110-403, www.hotelcelimar.com, info @hotelcelimar.com).

$$ Hotel Romàntic is family-run, old-fashioned-elegant, and quirky. Its 78 rooms (including some in the annex, Hotel de la Renaixença) are nothing special, but the whole place feels classic and classy—especially the plush lounge and bar (S-€72, Sb-€86, D-€102, Db-€115, €10 extra for balcony, includes breakfast, no air-con or elevator, free Wi-Fi, Sant Isidre 33, tel. 938-948-375, fax 938-114-129, www.hotelromantic.com, romantic@hotelromantic .com).

$$ El Xalet (as in "Chalet") is of a similar vintage, with a little less style and lower prices. They have 11 rooms in the main hotel and another 12 in their annex, Hotel Noucentista, up the street—both in fine old Modernista buildings (Db-€100, €25 extra for suite, includes breakfast, air-con, free Wi-Fi, Carrer Illa de Cuba 35, tel. 938-110-070, fax 938-945-579, www.elxalet.com, info@elxalet.com).

Montserrat

NEAR BARCELONA

Montserrat—the "serrated mountain"—rockets dramatically up from the valley floor northwest of Barcelona. With its unique rock formations, a dramatic mountaintop monastery (also called Montserrat), and spiritual connection with the Catalan people and their struggles, it's a popular day trip. This has been Catalunya's most important pilgrimage site for a thousand years. Hymns explain how the mountain

was carved by little angels with golden saws. Geologists blame nature at work.

Once upon a time, there was no mountain. A river flowed here, laying down silt that hardened into sedimentary layers of hard rock. Ten million years ago, the continents shifted, and the land around the rock massif sank, exposing this series of peaks that reach upward to 4,000 feet. Over time, erosion pocked the face with caves and cut vertical grooves near the top, creating the famous serrated look.

The monastery is nestled in the jagged peaks at 2,400 feet, but it seems higher because of the way the rocky massif rises out of nowhere. The air is certainly fresher than in Barcelona. In a quick day trip, you can view the mountain from its base, ride a funicular up to the top of the world, tour the basilica and museum, touch a Black Virgin's orb, hike down to a sacred cave, and listen to Gregorian chants by the world's oldest boys' choir.

Montserrat's monastery is Benedictine, and its 30 monks carry on its spiritual tradition. Since 1025 the slogan *"ora et labora"* ("prayer and work") has pretty much summed up life for a monk here.

The Benedictines welcome visitors—both pilgrims and tourists—and offer this travel tip: Please remember that the most important part of your Montserrat visit is not enjoying the architecture, but rather discovering the religious, cultural, historical, social, and environmental values that together symbolically express the life of the Catalan people.

Getting to Montserrat

Barcelona is connected to the valley below Montserrat by a convenient train; from there a cable car or rack railway (your choice) takes you up to the mountaintop. Both options are similar in cost

Tickets to Montserrat

Various combo-tickets cover your journey to Montserrat, as well as some of the sights you'll visit there. All begin with the train from Barcelona's Plaça d'Espanya, and include either the cable car or rack railway—you'll have to specify one or the other when you buy the ticket (same price for either option). You can't go one way and come back the other, unless you pay extra (about €5) for the leg that's not included in your ticket.

The basic option is to buy a **train ticket** to Montserrat (€16 round-trip, includes the cable car or rack railway to monastery, Eurailpass not valid, tel. 932-051-515, www.fgc.es). Note that if you buy this ticket in Barcelona, then decide at Montserrat that you want to use the funiculars, you can buy a €8.10 ticket covering both funiculars at the TI or at either funicular.

If you plan to do some sightseeing once at Montserrat, it makes sense to spend a little more on one of two combo-tickets from the train company: The €23.10 **Trans Montserrat** ticket includes your round-trip Metro ride in Barcelona to and from the train station, the train trip, the cable car or rack railway, unlimited trips on the two funiculars at Montserrat, and entry to the audiovisual presentation. The €38.45 **Tot Montserrat** ticket includes all of this, plus the good Museum of Montserrat and a self-service lunch. Both tickets are well-explained in the Barcelona TI's online shop (http://bcn shop.barcelonaturisme.com; look for them under the "Near Barcelona" tab).

If you plan to do it all, you'll save at least €5 with either of these combo-tickets. You can buy any of these tickets from the automated machines at Barcelona's Plaça d'Espanya Station (tourist officials are standing by in the morning to help you figure it out). To use your included round-trip Metro ride to get *to* the station, buy the ticket in advance at the Plaça de Catalunya TI in Barcelona, or at the uncrowded FGC La Molina office next to Plaça de Catalunya (Mon–Fri 10:00–14:00 & 16:30–20:30, Sat 10:00–14:00, closed Sun, Pelai 17–39 Triangle, tel. 933-664-553).

and take about the same amount of time (hourly trains, 1.5 hours each way from downtown Barcelona to the monastery). For ticket options, see the sidebar. Driving or taking the bus round out your options.

Train Plus Cable Car or Rack Railway

By Train: Trains leave hourly from Barcelona's Plaça d'Espanya to Montserrat. Take the Metro to Espanya, then follow signs showing a picture of a train to the FGC (Ferrocarrils de la Generalitat de Catalunya) underground station. Once there, look for train line R5 (direction: Manresa, departures at :36 past each hour).

You'll ride about an hour on the train. As you reach the base of the mountain, you have two options: Get out at Montserrat-Aeri for the cable car, or continue another few minutes to the next stop—Monistrol de Montserrat (or simply "Monistrol de M.")—for the rack railway. (You'll have to make this decision when you buy your ticket in Barcelona—see "Tickets to Montserrat" sidebar.)

Cable Car or Rack Train? For the sake of scenery and fun, I enjoy the little German-built cable car more than the rack railway. Departures are more frequent (4/hour rather than hourly on the railway), but because the cable car is small, you might have to wait a while to get on. Paying the extra €5 to do both isn't worthwhile.

By Cable Car, at the Montserrat-Aeri Stop: Departing the train, follow signs to the cable-car station (€5.40 one-way, €8.50

round-trip, covered by your train or combo-ticket, 4/hour, 5-minute trip, daily March–Oct 9:40–14:00 & 14:35–19:00, Nov–Feb 10:10–14:00 & 14:35–17:45—note the lunch break). Because the cable car is smaller than the train, don't linger or you might have to wait for the next car. On the way back down, cable cars depart from the monastery at :40 past the hour to make the Barcelona-bound trains leaving at :48 past the hour. In summer the last efficient departure is at 18:40 (off-season at 17:40). Although there's a later cable-car departure from the monastery (at 19:00, or 17:45 off-season), it entails almost an hour-long wait for the next Barcelona-bound train.

By Rack Railway (Cremallera), at the Monistrol de Montserrat Stop: From this stop you can catch the Cremallera rack railway up to the monastery (€5.15 one-way, €8.20 round-trip, cheaper off-season, covered by your train or combo-ticket, hourly, 20-minute trip, www.cremalleradmontserrat.com). On the return trip, this train departs the monastery at :15 past the hour (:22 past the hour on winter weekdays), allowing you to catch the Barcelona-bound train leaving Monistrol de Montserrat at :44 past the hour. The last convenient connection back to Barcelona leaves the monastery at 18:15 (or 20:15 in July–Aug). Confirm the schedule when you arrive, as specific times tend to change year to year. Note that there is one intermediate stop on this line (Monistrol-Vila, at a large parking garage), but—going in either direction—you want to stay on until the end of the line.

By Car or Bus

By Car: Once drivers get out of Barcelona (Road #82, then C-55), it's a short 30-minute drive to the base of the mountain, then a 10-minute series of switchbacks to the actual site (where you can find parking for €5/day). It may be easier to park your car down below and ride the cable car up.

By Bus: One bus per day connects downtown Barcelona directly to the monastery at Montserrat (departs from Viriat Street near Barcelona's Sants Station daily at 9:15, returns from the monastery to Barcelona at 18:00 June–Sept or at 17:00 Oct–May, €5 each way, one-hour trip depending on traffic). You can also take a four-hour bus tour offered by the Barcelona Guide Bureau (€40, leaves daily at 15:00 from Plaça Catalunya). However, since the other options are scenic, fun, and relatively easy, the only reason to take a bus is to avoid transfers.

Orientation to Montserrat

When you arrive at the base of the mountain, look up the rock face to find the cable-car line, the monastery near the top, and the tiny building midway up (marking the Sacred Cave).

However you make your way up to the Montserrat monastery, it's easy to get oriented once you arrive at the top. Everything is within a few minutes' walk of your entry point. All of the transit options—including the rack railway and cable car—converge at the big train station. Above those are both funicular stations: one up to the ridgetop, the other down to the Sacred Cave trail. Across the street is the TI, and above that (either straight up the stairs, or up the ramp around the left side) is the main square. To the right of the station, a long road leads along the cliff to the parking lot; a humble farmers market along here sells produce.

Crowd-Beating Tips: Arrive early or late, as tour groups mob the place midday. Crowds are less likely on weekdays and worst on Sundays.

Tourist Information

The square below the basilica houses a helpful TI, right across from the train station (daily from 9:00, closes just after last train heads down—roughly 18:15, or 20:15 in July–Aug, tel. 938-777-701, www.montserratvisita.com). Pick up the free map and get your questions answered. A good audioguide, available only at the TI, describes the general site and basilica, and also covers the Museum of Montserrat (€5, includes book). If you're a hiker, buy a hiking brochure here. Trails offer spectacular views (on clear days) to the Mediterranean and even (on clearer days) to the Pyrenees.

The audiovisual center (upstairs from the TI) provides some cultural and historical perspective. The lame interactive exhibition—nowhere near as exciting as the mountains and basilica outside—includes computer touch-screens and a short 20-minute video in English. Learn about the mountain's history, and get a glimpse into the daily lives of the monastery's resident monks (€2, covered by Trans Montserrat and Tot Montserrat combo-tickets, same hours as TI).

Self-Guided Spin Tour

From the monastery's main square, Plaça de Santa Maria, face the main facade and take this spin tour, moving from right to left: Like a good pilgrim, face Mary, the centerpiece of the facade. Below her to the left is St. Benedict, the sixth-century monk who established the rules that came to govern Montserrat's monastery. St. George, the symbol of Catalunya, is on the right (amid victims of Spain's Civil War).

Five arches line the base of the church. The one on the far right leads pilgrims to the high point of any visit, the Black Virgin (a.k.a. La Moreneta). The center arch leads into the basilica, and the arch second from left directs you to a small votive chapel filled with articles representing prayer requests or thanks.

Left of the basilica, the delicate arches mark the old monks' cloister. Beneath that are four trees planted by the monks, hoping to harvest only their symbolism (palm = martyrdom, cypress = eternal life, olive = peace, and laurel = victory). Next to the trees are a public library and a peaceful reading room. The big archway is the private entrance to the monastery. Then comes the modern hotel and, below that, the modern, white museum. Other buildings provide cells for pilgrims. The Sant Joan funicular lifts hikers up to the trailhead (you can see the tiny building at the top). From there you can take a number of fine hikes (described later). Another funicular station descends to the Sacred Cave. And, finally, five arches separate statues of founders of the great religious orders. Step over to the arches for a commanding view (on a clear day) of the Llobregat River, meandering all the way to the Mediterranean.

Sights in Montserrat

Basilica—Although there's been a church here since the 11th century, the present structure was built in the 1850s, and the facade only dates from 1968. The decor is Neo-Romanesque, so popular with the Romantic artists of the late 19th century. The basilica itself is ringed with interesting chapels, but the focus is on the Black Virgin sitting high above the main altar.

The History of Montserrat

The first hermit monks built huts at Montserrat around A.D. 900. By 1025, a monastery was founded. The Montserrat Escolania, or Choir School, soon followed, and is considered to be the oldest music school in Europe (they still perform).

Legend has it that in medieval times, some shepherd children saw lights and heard songs coming from the mountain. They traced the sounds to a cave (now called the Sacred Cave, or Santa Cova), where they found the Black Virgin statue (La Moreneta), making the monastery a pilgrim magnet.

In 1811 Napoleon's invading French troops destroyed Montserrat's buildings, though the Black Virgin, hidden away by monks, survived. Then, in the 1830s, the Spanish royalty—tired of dealing with pesky religious orders—dissolved the monasteries and convents.

But in the 1850s, the monks returned as part of Catalunya's (and Europe's) renewed Romantic appreciation for all things medieval and nationalistic. (Montserrat's revival coincided with other traditions born out of rejuvenated Catalan pride: the much-loved Football Club Barcelona; Barcelona's Palace of Catalan Music; and even the birth of local sparkling wine, *cava*.) Montserrat's basilica and monastery were reconstructed and became, once more, the strongly beating spiritual and cultural heart of the Catalan people.

Then came Franco, who wanted a monolithic Spain. To him Montserrat represented Catalan rebelliousness. During Franco's rule, the *sardana* dance was still illegally performed here (but with a different name), and literature was published in the outlawed Catalan language. In 1970, 300 intellectuals demonstrating for more respect for human rights in Spain were locked up in the monastery for several days by Franco's police.

But now Franco is history. The 1990s brought another phase of rebuilding (after a forest fire and rain damage), and the Montserrat community is thriving once again, unafraid to display its pride for the Catalan people, culture, and faith.

Montserrat's top attraction is **La Moreneta,** the small wood statue of the Black Virgin, discovered in the Sacred Cave in the 12th century. Legend says she was carved by St. Luke (the Gospel writer and supposed artist), brought to Spain by St. Peter, hidden away in the cave during the Moorish invasions, and miraculously discovered by shepherd children. (Carbon dating says she's 800 years old.) While George is the patron saint of Catalunya, La Moreneta is its patroness, having been crowned as such by the pope in 1881. "Moreneta" is usually translated as "black" in English, but the Spanish name actually means "tanned." The statue was originally lighter, but darkened over the centuries from candle smoke, humidity, and the natural aging of its original varnish. Pilgrims shuffle down a long, ornate passage leading alongside the church for their few moments alone with the virgin (free, daily 8:00–10:30 & 12:00–18:30, plus 19:30–20:15 in summer, www .abadiamontserrat.net). The church itself has longer hours and daily services (Mass at 11:00, vespers at 18:45).

Join the line of pilgrims (along the right side of the church). Though Mary is behind a protective glass case, the royal orb she cradles in her hands is exposed. Pilgrims touch Mary's orb with one hand and hold their other hand up to show that they accept Jesus. Newlyweds in particular seek Mary's blessing.

Immediately after La Moreneta, turn right into the delightful Neo-Romanesque prayer chapel, where worshippers sit behind the Virgin and continue to pray. The ceiling, painted in the Modernista style in 1898 by Joan Llimona, shows Jesus and Mary high in heaven. The trail connecting Catalunya with heaven seems to lead through these serrated mountains. The figures depicted lower are people symbolizing Catalan history and culture.

You'll leave by walking along the Ave Maria Path (along the outside of the church), which thoughtfully integrates nature and the basilica. Thousands of colorful votive candles are all busy helping the devout with their prayers. Before you leave the inner courtyard and head out into the main square, pop in to the humble little room with the many votive offerings. This is where people leave personal belongings (wedding dresses, baby's baptism outfits, wax replicas of body parts in need of healing, and so on) as part of a prayer request or as a thanks for divine intercession.

Museum of Montserrat—The bright, shiny, and cool collection of paintings and artifacts was mostly donated by devout Catalan Catholics. While it's nothing really earth-shaking, you'll enjoy an air-conditioned wander past lots of antiquities and fine artwork. Head upstairs first to see some lesser-known works by the likes of Picasso, El Greco, Caravaggio, Monet, Renoir, Pissarro, Degas, John Singer Sargent, and some local Modernista artists. One gallery shows how artists have depicted the Black Virgin of Montserrat over the centuries in many different styles. There's even a small Egyptian section, with a sarcophagus and mummy. Down on the main floor, you'll see ecclesiastical gear, a good icon collection, and more paintings, including—at the very end—a Dalí painting, some Picasso sketches and prints, and a Miró (€6.50, covered by Tot

Montserrat combo-ticket; July–Aug daily 10:00–19:00; Sept–June Mon–Fri 10:00–17:45, Sat–Sun 10:00–18:45; tel. 938-777-745).

Sant Joan Funicular and Hikes—This funicular climbs 820 feet above the monastery in five minutes (€4.50 one-way, €7.20 round-trip, covered by Trans Montserrat and Tot Montserrat combo-tickets, goes every 20 minutes, more often with demand). At the top of the funicular, you are at the starting point of a 20-minute walk that takes you to the Sant Joan Chapel (follow sign for *Ermita de St. Joan*). Other hikes also begin at the trailhead by the funicular (get details from TI before you ascend; basic map with suggested hikes posted by upper funicular station). For a quick and easy chance to get out into nature, simply ride up and follow the most popular hike, a 45-minute mostly downhill loop through mountain scenery back to the monastery. To take this route, go left from the funicular station; the trail—marked *Monestir de Montserrat*—will first go up to a rocky crest before heading downhill.

Sacred Cave (Santa Cova)—The Moreneta was originally discovered in the Sacred Cave (or Sacred Grotto), a 40-minute hike down from the monastery (then another 50 minutes back up). The path (c. 1900) was designed by devoted and patriotic Modernista architects, including Gaudí and Josep Puig i Cadafalch. It's lined with Modernista statues depicting scenes from the life of Christ. While the original Black Virgin statue is now in the basilica, a replica sits in the cave. A three-minute funicular ride cuts 20 minutes off the hike (€1.80 one-way, €2.90 round-trip, covered by Trans Montserrat and Tot Montserrat combo-tickets, goes every 20 minutes, more often with demand).

If you're here late in the afternoon, check the funicular schedule before you head into the Sacred Cave to make sure you don't miss the final ride down. Missing the last ride could mean catching a train back to Barcelona later than you had planned.

Choir Concert—Montserrat's Escolania, or Choir School, has been training voices for centuries. Fifty young boys, who live and study in the monastery itself, make up the choir, which performs daily except Saturday (Mon–Fri at 13:00, Sun–Thu at 18:45, and Sun also at 12:00, choir on vacation late June–late Aug). The boys sing for only 10 minutes, the basilica is jam-packed, and it's likely you'll see almost nothing. Also note that if you attend the evening performance, you'll miss the last funicular down the mountain.

Sleeping in Montserrat

An overnight here gets you monastic peace and a total break from the modern crowds. There are ample rustic cells for pilgrim visitors, but tourists might prefer this place:

$$ Hotel Abat Cisneros, a three-star hotel with 82 rooms and all the comforts, is low-key and appropriate for a sanctuary (Sb-€39–64, Db-€68–111, price depends on season, includes breakfast, half- and full-board available, elevator, pay Internet access, free Wi-Fi, tel. 938-777-701, fax 938-777-724, www.abadiamontserrat.cat, reserves@larsa-montserrat.cat).

Eating in Montserrat

Montserrat is designed to feed hordes of pilgrims and tourists. You'll find a cafeteria along the main street (across from the train station) and more eateries (including a grocery store and bar with simple sandwiches) where the road curves on its way up to the basilica. Or pack a picnic from Barcelona.

PRACTICALITIES

This section covers just the basics on traveling in Spain (for much more information, see the latest edition of *Rick Steves' Spain*). You can find free advice on specific topics at www.ricksteves.com/tips.

Money

Spain uses the euro currency: 1 euro (€) = about $1.25. To convert prices in euros to dollars, add about 25 percent: €20 = about $25, €50 = about $65. (Check www.oanda.com for the latest exchange rates.)

The standard way for travelers to get euros is to withdraw money from a cash machine (called a *cajero automático*) using a debit or credit card, ideally with a Visa or MasterCard logo. Before departing, call your bank or credit-card company: Confirm that your card will work overseas, ask about international transaction fees, and alert them that you'll be making withdrawals in Europe.

To keep your valuables safe, wear a money belt. But if you do lose your credit or debit card, report the loss immediately to the respective global customer-assistance centers. Call these 24-hour US numbers collect: Visa (410/581-9994), MasterCard (636/722-7111), and American Express (623/492-8427).

Phoning

Smart travelers use the telephone to reserve or reconfirm rooms, reserve restaurants, get directions, research transportation connections, confirm tour times, phone home, and lots more.

To call Spain from the US or Canada: Dial 011-34 and then the local number. (The 011 is our international access code, and 34 is Spain's country code.)

To call Spain from a European country: Dial 00-34 followed by the local number. (The 00 is Europe's international access code.)

To call within Spain: Just dial the local number.

To call from Spain to another country: Dial 00 followed by the country code (for example, 1 for the US or Canada), then the area code and number. If calling European countries which have phone numbers that begin with 0, you'll usually have to omit the 0 when you dial.

Tips on Phoning: To make calls in Spain, you can buy two different types of phone cards—international or insertable—sold locally at newsstands. Cheap international phone cards, which work with a scratch-to-reveal PIN code at any phone, allow you to call home to the US for pennies a minute, and also work for domestic calls within Spain. Insertable phone cards, which must be inserted into public pay phones, are reasonable for calls within Spain (and work for international calls as well, but not as cheaply as the international phone cards). Calling from your hotel-room phone is usually expensive, unless you use an international phone card. A mobile phone—whether an American one that works in Spain, or a European one you buy when you arrive—is handy, but can be pricey. For more on phoning, see www.ricksteves.com/phoning.

Emergency Telephone Numbers in Spain: For **police** help, dial 091. To summon an **ambulance**, call 112. For passport problems, call the **US Embassy** (in Madrid, tel. 915-872-240, after-hours emergency tel. 915-872-200) or the **Canadian Embassy** (in Madrid, tel. 914-233-250). For other concerns, get advice from your hotel.

Making Hotel Reservations

To ensure the best value, I recommend reserving rooms in advance, particularly during peak season. Email the hotelier with the following key pieces of information: number and type of rooms; number of nights; date of arrival; date of departure; and any special requests. (For a sample form, see www.ricksteves.com/reservation.) Use the European style for writing dates: day/month/year. For example, for a two-night stay in July, you could request: "1 double room for 2 nights, arrive 16/07/11, depart 18/07/11." Hoteliers typically ask for your credit-card number as a deposit.

Given the economic downturn, hoteliers are willing and eager to make a deal. I'd suggest emailing several hotels to ask for their best price. Comparison-shop and make your choice.

In general, hotel prices can soften if you do any of the following: offer to pay cash, stay at least three nights, mention this book or travel off-season. You can also try asking for a cheaper room (for example, with a bathroom down the hall), or offer to skip breakfast.

Eating

By our standards, Spaniards eat late, having lunch—their biggest meal of the day—around 13:00-16:00, and dinner starting about 21:00. At restaurants, you can dine with tourists at 20:00, or with Spaniards if you wait until later.

For a fun early dinner at a bar, build a light meal out of tapas—small appetizer-sized portions of seafood, salads, meat-filled pastries, deep-fried tasties, and so on. Many of these are displayed behind glass, and you can point to what you want. Tapas typically cost about €2 apiece, but can run up to €10 for seafood. While the smaller "tapa" size (which comes on a saucer-size plate) is handiest for maximum tasting opportunities, many bars sell only larger sizes: the *ración* (full portion, on a dinner plate) and *media-ración* (half-size portion). *Jamón* (hah-MOHN), an air-dried ham similar to prosciutto, is a Spanish staple. Other key terms include *bocadillo* (baguette sandwich), *frito* (fried), *a la plancha* (grilled), *queso* (cheese), *tortilla* (omelet), and *surtido* (assortment).

Many bars have three price tiers, which should be clearly posted: It's cheapest to eat or drink while standing at the bar (*barra*), slightly more to sit at a table inside (*mesa* or *salón*), and most expensive to sit outside *(terraza)*. Wherever you are, be assertive or you'll never be served. *Por favor* (please) grabs the attention of the server or bartender. If you're having tapas, you don't have to pay throughout the meal; the bartender keeps track. When you're ready to leave, ask for the bill: *"¿La cuenta?"* To tip for a few tapas, round up to the nearest euro; for a full meal, tip about 5 to 10 percent for good service.

Transportation

By Train and Bus: For train schedules, check www.renfe.es. Since trains can sell out, it's smart to buy your tickets a day in advance at a travel agency (easiest), at the train station (can be crowded; be sure you're in the right line), or online (at www.renfe.es; when asked for your Spanish national ID number, enter your passport number). Futuristic, high-speed trains (such as AVE) can be priced differently according to their time of departure. To see if a railpass could save you money, check www.ricksteves.com/rail.

Buses pick up where the trains don't go, reaching even small villages. But because routes are operated by various competing companies, it can be tricky to pin down schedules (inquire at local bus stations or TIs).

By Plane: Consider covering long distances on a budget flight, which can be cheaper than a train or bus ride. For flights within Spain, check out www.vueling.com, www.iberia.com, or www.spanair.com; and to compare several airlines, see www.skyscanner.net.

By Car: It's cheaper to arrange most car rentals from the US. For tips on your insurance options, see www.ricksteves .com/cdw. Bring an International Driving Permit (available at your local AAA office) and your driver's license. For route planning, try www.viamichelin.com. Freeways come with tolls (about $4/hr), but save lots of time. A car is a worthless headache in cities—park it safely (get tips from your hotel). As break-ins are common, be sure all of your valuables are out of sight and locked in the trunk, or even better, with you or in your hotel room.

Helpful Hints

Theft Alert: Spain has particularly hardworking pickpockets. Assume beggars are pickpockets and any scuffle is simply a distraction by a team of thieves. If you stop for any commotion or show, put your hands in your pockets before someone else does. Better yet, wear a money belt.

Time: Spain uses the 24-hour clock. It's the same through 12:00 noon, then keep going: 13:00, 14:00, and so on. Spain, like most of continental Europe, is six/nine hours ahead of the East/ West Coasts of the US.

Siesta and Paseo: Many Spaniards (especially in rural areas) still follow the traditional siesta schedule: From around 13:00 to 16:00, many businesses close as people go home for a big lunch with their family. Then they head back to work (and shops re-open) from about 16:00 to 20:00. (Many bigger stores stay open all day long, especially in cities.) Then, after a late dinner, whole families pour out of their apartments to enjoy the cool of the evening, stroll through the streets, and greet their neighbors—a custom called the paseo. Tourists are welcome to join this people-parade.

Sights: Major attractions can be swamped with visitors; carefully read and follow this book's crowd-beating tips (visit at quieter times of day, or—where possible—reserve ahead). At many churches, a modest dress code is encouraged and sometimes required (no bare shoulders, miniskirts, or shorts).

Holidays and Festivals: Spain celebrates many holidays, which can close sights and attract crowds (book hotel rooms ahead). For more on holidays and festivals, check Spain's website: www.spain.info. For a simple list showing major—though not all—events, see www.ricksteves.com/festivals.

Numbers and Stumblers: What Americans call the second floor of a building is the first floor in Europe. Europeans write dates as day/month/year, so Christmas is 25/12/11. Commas are decimal points and vice versa—a dollar and a half is 1,50, and there are 5.280 feet in a mile. Spain uses the metric system: A kilogram is 2.2 pounds; a liter is about a quart; and a kilometer is six-tenths of a mile.

Resources from Rick Steves

This Snapshot guide is excerpted from the latest edition of *Rick Steves' Spain,* which is one of more than 30 titles in my series of guidebooks on European travel. I also produce a public television series, *Rick Steves' Europe,* and a public radio show, *Travel with Rick Steves.* My website, www.ricksteves.com, offers free travel information, free vodcasts and podcasts of my shows, free audio tours of major sights in Europe (for you to download onto an iPod or other MP3 player), a Graffiti Wall for travelers' comments, guidebook updates, my travel blog, an online travel store, and information on European railpasses and our tours of Europe.

Additional Resources

Tourist Information: www.spain.info
Passports and Red Tape: www.travel.state.gov
Travel Insurance Tips: www.ricksteves.com/insurance
Packing List: www.ricksteves.com/packlist
Cheap Flights: www.skyscanner.net
Airplane Carry-on Restrictions: www.tsa.gov/travelers
Updates for This Book: www.ricksteves.com/update

How Was Your Trip?

If you'd like to share your tips, concerns, and discoveries after using this book, please fill out the survey at www.ricksteves.com /feedback. Thanks in advance—it helps a lot.

Spanish Survival Phrases

Spanish has a guttural sound similar to the J in Baja California. In the
phonetics, the symbol for this clearing-your-throat sound is the italicize

English	Spanish	Phonetics
Good day.	**Buenos días.**	bway-nohs **dee**-ahs
Do you speak English?	**¿Habla Usted inglés?**	ah-blah oo-**stehd** een-**glays**
Yes. / No.	**Sí. / No.**	see / noh
I (don't) understand.	**(No) comprendo.**	(noh) kohm-**prehn**-doh
Please.	**Por favor.**	por fah-**bor**
Thank you.	**Gracias.**	**grah**-thee-ahs
I'm sorry.	**Lo siento.**	loh see-**ehn**-toh
Excuse me.	**Perdóneme.**	pehr-**doh**-nay-may
(No) problem.	**(No) problema.**	(noh) proh-**blay**-mah
Good.	**Bueno.**	**bway**-noh
Goodbye.	**Adiós.**	ah-dee-**ohs**
one / two	**uno / dos**	**oo**-noh / dohs
three / four	**tres / cuatro**	trays / **kwah**-troh
five / six	**cinco / seis**	**theen**-koh / says
seven / eight	**siete / ocho**	see-**eh**-tay / **oh**-choh
nine / ten	**nueve / diez**	**nway**-bay / dee-**ayth**
How much is it?	**¿Cuánto cuesta?**	**kwahn**-toh **kway**-stah
Write it?	**¿Me lo escribe?**	may loh ay-**skree**-bay
Is it free?	**¿Es gratis?**	ays **grah**-tees
Is it included?	**¿Está incluido?**	ay-**stah** een-kloo-**ee**-doh
Where can I buy / find...?	**¿Dónde puedo comprar / encontrar...?**	**dohn**-day **pway**-doh kohm-**prar** / ayn-kohn-**tra**
I'd like / We'd like...	**Quiero / Queremos...**	kee-**ehr**-oh / kehr-**ay**-mohs
...a room.	**...una habitación.**	**oo**-nah ah-bee-tah-thee-**oh**
...a ticket to ___.	**...un billete para ___.**	oon bee-**yeh**-tay **pah**-rah
Is it possible?	**¿Es posible?**	ays poh-**see**-blay
Where is...?	**¿Dónde está...?**	**dohn**-day ay-**stah**
...the train station	**...la estación de trenes**	lah ay-stah-thee-**ohn** day tr
...the bus station	**...la estación de autobuses**	lah ay-stah-thee-**ohn** day ow-toh-**boo**-says
...the tourist information office	**...la oficina de turismo**	lah oh-fee-**thee**-nah day too-**rees**-moh
Where are the toilets?	**¿Dónde están los servicios?**	**dohn**-day ay-**stahn** lohs sehr-**bee**-thee-ohs
men	**hombres, caballeros**	**ohm**-brays, kah-bah-**yay**-ro
women	**mujeres, damas**	moo-**heh**-rays, **dah**-mahs
left / right	**izquierda / derecha**	eeth-kee-**ehr**-dah / day-**ray**
straight	**derecho**	day-**ray**-choh
When do you open / close?	**¿A qué hora abren / cierran?**	ah kay **oh**-rah **ah**-brehn / thee-**ay**-rahn
At what time?	**¿A qué hora?**	ah kay **oh**-rah
Just a moment.	**Un momento.**	oon moh-**mehn**-toh
now / soon / later	**ahora / pronto / más tarde**	ah-**oh**-rah / **prohn**-toh / mahs **tar**-day
today / tomorrow	**hoy / mañana**	oy / mahn-**yah**-nah

In the Restaurant

I'd like / We'd like...	**Quiero / Queremos...**	kee-**ehr**-oh / kehr-**ay**-mohs
...to reserve...	**...reservar...**	ray-sehr-**bar**
...a table for one / two.	**...una mesa para uno / dos.**	oo-nah **may**-sah **pah**-rah oo-noh / dohs
Non-smoking.	**No fumador.**	noh foo-mah-**dohr**
Is this table free?	**¿Está esta mesa libre?**	ay-**stah** ay-stah **may**-sah lee-bray
The menu (in English), please.	**La carta (en inglés), por favor.**	lah **kar**-tah (ayn een-**glays**) por fah-**bor**
service (not) included	**servicio (no) incluido**	sehr-**bee**-thee-oh (noh) een-kloo-**ee**-doh
cover charge	**precio de entrada**	**pray**-thee-oh day ayn-**trah**-dah
to go	**para llevar**	**pah**-rah yay-**bar**
with / without	**con / sin**	kohn / seen
and / or	**y / o**	ee / oh
menu (of the day)	**menú (del día)**	may-**noo** (dayl **dee**-ah)
specialty of the house	**especialidad de la casa**	ay-spay-thee-ah-lee-**dahd** day lah **kah**-sah
tourist menu	**menú turístico**	meh-**noo** too-**ree**-stee-koh
combination plate	**plato combinado**	**plah**-toh kohm-bee-**nah**-doh
appetizers	**tapas**	**tah**-pahs
bread	**pan**	pahn
cheese	**queso**	**kay**-soh
sandwich	**bocadillo**	boh-kah-**dee**-yoh
soup	**sopa**	**soh**-pah
salad	**ensalada**	ayn-sah-**lah**-dah
meat	**carne**	**kar**-nay
poultry	**aves**	**ah**-bays
fish	**pescado**	pay-**skah**-doh
seafood	**marisco**	mah-**ree**-skoh
fruit	**fruta**	**froo**-tah
vegetables	**verduras**	behr-**doo**-rahs
dessert	**postres**	**poh**-strays
tap water	**agua del grifo**	**ah**-gwah dayl **gree**-foh
mineral water	**agua mineral**	**ah**-gwah mee-nay-**rahl**
milk	**leche**	**lay**-chay
(orange) juice	**zumo (de naranja)**	**thoo**-moh (day nah-**rahn**-hah)
coffee	**café**	kah-**feh**
tea	**té**	tay
wine	**vino**	**bee**-noh
red / white	**tinto / blanco**	**teen**-toh / **blahn**-koh
glass / bottle	**vaso / botella**	**bah**-soh / boh-**tay**-yah
beer	**cerveza**	thehr-**bay**-thah
Cheers!	**¡Salud!**	sah-**lood**
More. / Another.	**Más. / Otro.**	mahs / **oh**-troh
The same.	**El mismo.**	ehl **mees**-moh
The bill, please.	**La cuenta, por favor.**	lah **kwayn**-tah por fah-**bor**
tip	**propina**	proh-**pee**-nah
Delicious!	**¡Delicioso!**	day-lee-thee-**oh**-soh

For hundreds more pages of survival phrases for your trip to Spain, check out *Rick Steves' Spanish Phrase Book.*

Audio Europe

Free mobile app (and podcast)

With the **Rick Steves Audio Europe** app, your iPhone or smartphone becomes a powerful travel tool.

This exciting app organizes Rick's entire audio library by country—giving you a playlist of all his audio walking tours, radio interviews, and travel tips for wherever you're going in Europe.

Let the experts Rick interviews enrich your understanding. Let Rick's self-guided tours amplify your guidebook. With Rick in your ear, Europe gets even better.

Thanks Facebook fans for submitting photos while on location! From top: John Kuijper in Florence, Brenda Mamer with her mother in Rome, Angel Capobianco in London, and Alyssa Passey with her friend in Paris.

Find out more at ricksteves.com/audioeurope

▸ Plan Your Trip

Browse thousands of articles and a wealth of money-saving tips for planning your dream trip. You'll find up-to-date information on Europe's best destinations, packing smart, getting around, finding rooms, staying healthy, avoiding scams and more.

▸ Eurail Passes

Find out, step-by-step, if a railpass makes sense for your trip—and how to avoid buying more than you need. Get a bunch of free extras!

▸ Graffiti Wall & Travelers' Helpline

Learn, ask, share—our online community of savvy travelers is a great resource for first-time travelers to Europe, as well as seasoned pros.

Rick Steves' Europe Through the Back Door, Inc.

urn your travel dreams into affordable reality

▶ Free Audio Tours & Travel Newsletter

Get your nose out of this guide book and focus on what you'll be seeing with Rick's free audio tours of the greatest sights in Paris, London, Rome, Florence and Venice.

Subscribe to our free Travel News e-newsletter, and get monthly articles from Rick on what's happening in Europe.

▶ Great Gear from Rick's Travel Store

Pack light and right—on a budget—with Rick's custom-designed carry-on bags, roll-aboards, day packs, travel accessories, guidebooks, journals, maps and DVDs of his TV shows.

130 Fourth Avenue North, PO Box 2009 • Edmonds, WA 98020 USA
Phone: (425) 771-8303 • Fax: (425) 771-0833 • www.ricksteves.com

Rick Steves

www.ricksteves.com

EUROPE GUIDES

Best of Europe
Eastern Europe
Europe Through the Back Door

COUNTRY GUIDES

Croatia & Slovenia
England
France
Germany
Great Britain
Ireland
Italy
Portugal
Scandinavia
Spain
Switzerland

CITY & REGIONAL GUIDES

Amsterdam, Bruges & Brussels
Athens & the Peloponnese
Budapest
Florence & Tuscany
Istanbul
London
Paris
Prague & the Czech Republic
Provence & the French Riviera
Rome
Venice
Vienna, Salzburg & Tirol

SNAPSHOT GUIDES

Barcelona
Berlin
Bruges & Brussels
Copenhagen & the Best of
 Denmark
Dublin
Dubrovnik
Hill Towns of Central Italy
Italy's Cinque Terre
Krakow, Warsaw & Gdansk
Lisbon
Madrid & Toledo
Munich, Bavaria & Salzburg
Naples & the Amalfi Coast
Northern Ireland
Norway
Scotland
Sevilla, Granada & Southern Spain
Stockholm

TRAVEL CULTURE

Europe 101
European Christmas
Postcards from Europe
Travel as a Political Act

Rick Steves guidebooks are published by Avalon Travel,
a member of the Perseus Books Group.

NOW AVAILABLE: eBOOKS, APPS, DVDS, & BLU-RAY

eBOOKS

Most guides available as eBooks from Amazon, Barnes & Noble, Borders, Apple iBook and Sony eReader, beginning January 2011

RICK STEVES' EUROPE DVDs

Austria & the Alps
Eastern Europe, Israel & Egypt
England & Wales
European Travel Skills & Specials
France
Germany, Benelux & More
Greece & Turkey
Iran
Ireland & Scotland
Italy's Cities
Italy's Countryside
Rick Steves' European Christmas
Scandinavia
Spain & Portugal

BLU-RAY

Celtic Charms
Eastern Europe Favorites
European Christmas
Italy Through the Back Door
Surprising Cities of Europe

PHRASE BOOKS & DICTIONARIES

French
French, Italian & German
German
Italian
Portuguese
Spanish

JOURNALS

Rick Steves' Pocket Travel Journal
Rick Steves' Travel Journal

APPS

Rick Steves' Ancient Rome Tour
Rick Steves' Historic Paris Walk
Rick Steves' Louvre Tour
Rick Steves' Orsay Museum Tour
Rick Steves' St. Peter's Basilica Tour
Rick Steves' Versailles

PLANNING MAPS

Britain, Ireland & London
Europe
France & Paris
Germany, Austria & Switzerland
Ireland
Italy
Spain & Portugal